BEYOND BORDERS

ニューヨークタイムズ世界見聞

Edited with Notes and Exercises
by
Rume KITA
and
Keith Wesley ADAMS

EIHŌSHA

Beyond Borders

by

Eihōsha

PRINTED IN JAPAN

は じ め に

　シリーズでお届けしている New York Times の新しい読解テキストが出来上がりました．ここ数年の記事の中から，皆さんに読んでいただきたい 12 編を選び，タイトルを Beyond Borders としました．

　タイトルの Borders は，国境という意味だけでなく，経済や教育や産業などにおけるあらゆる意味での境界，人々の生活の中の物理的な，あるいは心理的，倫理的な境界線をさす言葉です．現代社会においては，人も物もやすやすと国境を越えて移動し，古いものは既成の境界を越えて新しい製品や技術に変革してゆきます．そして人々のニーズや価値観や意識が変わり，新しいトレンドが生まれます．12 編の記事は，Border を超えた人々，超えることに戸惑う人々，引き返そうとする人々，Border の手前でさらなる未来を考える人々のレポートです．

　カテゴリー I には，プラスティック製品やプラスティックごみをこれ以上増やすまいとする人々の倫理観や国の取り組みについての記事を収めました．皆さんの日常生活と比較しながら読んでください．

　カテゴリー II は，先進国の産業や思惑が国境を超え，途上国の人々の生活や健康を脅かしている現状です．門戸を開いて欧米の廃棄物や食生活を受け入れた結果を見てみましょう．弱者の生活が元に戻ることはあるのでしょうか．

　III は学生の皆さんに身近な教育現場の話題です．インターネットの利用が一線を越えると，人権が脅かされたり倫理観が麻痺する現状が報告されています．

　IV は，旅行や出産という明確な目的を持って国境を超える人々のレポートです．人生を豊かにするための移動は果たして正しい選択なのか，あるいはエゴイストの論理なのか．

　V は先端技術の功罪です．人間の代わりにタブレットやロボットがコミュニケーションの相手となる未来は明るいのでしょうか．あるいは，クローンとして生き返るペットは飼い主に幸せをもたらすのでしょうか．

　VI は新しい食生活の提案です．食品ロスを出さない取り組みや最新の技術で生まれる食品が人々にどのような充足感を与えられるのかを読みましょう．

　記事の選定を終えてタイトルに Borders という言葉を使うことを決め，同僚の Keith Wesley Adams 氏と共に作業を始めようとしたまさにその時，コロナウイルスが蔓延し始め，数ヶ月で世界の様相は一変しました．記事で描かれたような，簡単に人や物が国境を越えることは許されなくなり，記事では行き過ぎだと批判的に書かれている IT 技術が，新たな生活や教育や医療の必需品としてますます注目を浴びるようになりました．在宅生活が長引いたせいで，トレンドに逆行するようにプラスティックごみがさらに増え，逆に，懸念されてきた大気や海は綺麗になりました．日常の変化に伴い食生活が変わり，在宅生活を癒すペットは存在感を増しました．数ヶ月前までとはまた違う境界線上にいま私たちはいるのかもしれません．そしてコロナ後には世界の潮流はどう変化するのでしょう．新たに出現するであろう Borders を今後私たちは見定める必要がありそ

うです．

　今回は Pre-reading，Post-reading ともにリサーチやディスカッションのアクティビティを増やし，単に語彙力と読解力の向上を狙うだけでなく，多角的に調べたり考えたりすることによって記事をより身近なものとして捉えられるように企画しました．Pre-reading と Post-reading は Adams 氏の手によるものです．

　企画・編集作業におきましては今回も英宝社の下村幸一氏にたいへんお世話になりました．自由に仕事をさせていただき，的確なアドバイスと丁寧な対応で支えていただきましたことを心より感謝申し上げます．

2020 年　盛夏

喜多　留女

Preface - Beyond Borders
Keith Wesley Adams

We live on the edge of many borders: agricultural, biological, educational, geographical, technological, and the border of survival itself. Some of these borders are invisible, but we cross them anyway. Some of them should have guards on duty, moral guards, questioning our actions, foreseeing consequences, but we live in an age in which progress seems unstoppable and we are beyond the border of what is acceptable before we even realize it. We face the deep questions after the reality sets in. This book aims to look at some of these transnational issues that are affecting us, to help us understand where we are and consider whether we should cross those frontiers or turn back.

Capitalism is based on a concept of a borderless world with endless growth. The natural world, however, has limits which we may not go beyond if we want to survive. Sadly modern society, believing we can escape these boundaries through science and new discoveries, has ignored these red lines, resulting in tens of millions of metric tons of plastic waste in our oceans and landfills infiltrating and poisoning our food chain. Necessity is the mother of invention, and humans are creative in finding alternative ways, inventing new kinds of biodegradable plastic or going back to reusable containers, or living a plastic free life, like Crystal Ambrose (Unit 1). She, however, is not the mass. Our leaders refuse to give up their wealthy borders. Yet, quite beyond the borders of our expectations, it is governments in poorer countries, like Rwanda that are leading the way in the banning of plastic (Unit 2). The very reason they are able to enforce such laws is because the horrors of the Rwandan genocide went beyond acceptable limits of lawlessness, and the people are more than willing to obey draconian rules to avoid such terrifying chaos.

Similarly beyond the borders of our expectations, one of the new world centers of obesity is Kenya (Unit 3), where rapid economic growth means many people are moving beyond the borders of their traditional healthy, if hard, lifestyle and diet, and acquiring both the fast food and sedentary lifestyle of the developed world. Across Africa, quick development is making the dividing line between severe under-nutrition and over-nutrition a very thin line, revealing both extremes of malnutrition. Increasingly, the boundary lines of health are crossed where development and under-development mix in South East Asia, where old style lax environmental laws allow for importation of the developed world's e-waste. (Unit 4). Most of the West's used computers and smartphones are dumped in countries like Thailand, where poor illegal immigrants break them down with tiny hammers and bare hands, breathing in toxic fumes as they heat components to extract the rare minerals, leaving behind a highly polluted paradise.

Technology has also crossed into the frontiers of education, going beyond the borders of what is acceptable and legal. Western Universities find themselves flooded with essays their students bought online from countries as disparate as Kenya, India and the Ukraine (Unit 5). Extremely lucrative for writers in poor countries, the worldwide online "cheating" industry has made it near impossible to detect if a student's work is their own. China, on the other hand, has made it impossible for students to cheat or even slack off for a brief moment in their studies by bringing technology into the classroom in the form of live streaming cameras (Unit 6). With their every movement and stifled yawn caught on an immediately publicized surveillance system, Chinese students feel they are in a zoo, their creativity crushed and open to the prey of potential psychopaths.

Tourism has long reached the limits of where it can go. Climate change, the birth child of capitalism and technology has made everything from the ends of the world to the extinction of species tourist destinations as last chance travelers wish to see things before they disappear (Unit 7). Ironically crossing another moral border, such tourism may both hasten the destruction and simultaneously preserve what it visits. Medical and birth tourism now change the very reasons of travel. Wishing safer and cheaper hospitals, Chinese travel to Canada (Unit 8) to take advantage of its automatic citizenship rules, making it easier for their family to cross national borderlines and immigrate to a less authoritarian country.

Medicine and technology have also gone beyond the borderline of what is human and who gets human help. While high tech pushes it computers into schools, its CEOs put their children into schools without computers. Human contact has become a luxury. Unable to afford real social workers, companies now provide online "care coaches" in the form of robotic cat avatars in poor communities (Unit 9), while the extremely wealthy can have their real cats cloned (Unit 10) and brought back to life. If that alone does not cross enough moral boundaries, Chinese companies at the forefront of cloning, think it will soon be possible to transplant memories from original pets into the cloned one.

Our food is also crossing many of these similar technological and moral borders, often for good reasons. Due dates are questionable limits at best. Set up for the benefit of protecting consumers from illness, they result in 1.3 million tons of perfectly good food being thrown away each year. By selling such food at 60% off in supermarket "Happy hours," Finland thinks it has found a way to lose less money by extending limits through an anti-waste ethos. (Unit 11) Similarly, wasteful and unhealthy meat is having its realm crossed. New vegetarian substitutes have blurred the boundaries of taste, winning over even meat lovers in fast food restaurants. (Unit 12). Capable of reducing both heart disease and the large carbon footprint of raising animals, new plant based burgers have the beef industry in the U.S. scared, and trying to erect new legal boundaries.

This is the book in a nutshell: a huge variety of physical and moral borders are being reached, crossed and reestablished in our daily journey on this planet. There is a story called the 100th monkey, in which a monkey on an island learns to wash its food. It teaches another monkey, and another until all the monkeys on the island wash their food. Yet, somehow without any direct transmission, monkeys on all the surrounding islands suddenly begin washing their food before eating. It seems some crucial borderline of awareness was crossed in which a critical mass of consciousness was reached. We are going beyond so many borders, and stand on the very borderline of survival. Let's hope that we go beyond the critical mass of awareness that helps us make intelligent crossings into new lands and find ways that allow us to pull back from those borders that harm us.

Once again, my colleague, Rume Kita has chosen a wealth of fascinating articles from the New York Times and is the real force behind the book, organizing everything from contracts to final editing in addition to translations and explanations in Japanese. I, as always, provide the pre and post reading activities in the text, headings, and summaries and answers for the teacher's book. This time we have done our best to provide new forms of activities using maps and graphs and including research questions as well as discussion questions to aid in the over all learning process. We hope you enjoy.

◆ CONTENTS ◆

V. Technology: Transportation to or from Happiness?

VI. The Future Horizons of Foods

Beyond Borders

I

Getting Beyond the Boundaries of Plastic

Unit 1
A Life Without Plastic

By Steven Kurutz   Feb. 16, 2019

A: Crossword

Match the words in the Word Bank to their descriptions to fill in the crossword.

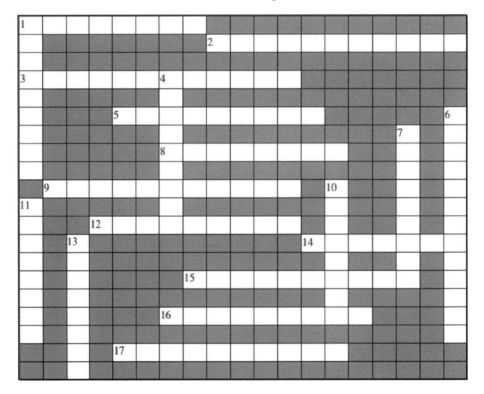

Word Bank

Advocacy	Albatross	Alternatives	Awareness	Bisphenol A*	Coalition
Conscious	Discarded	Disposable	Epiphany	Embraced	Emphasize
Indispensable	Millennials	Mission	Navigate	Refillable	Reusable

*Include space when filling in crossword.

Across
1. (n.) Active support of an idea or a cause.
2. (n.) Generation Y. People born within the years 1981-1996.
3. (n.) Other choices or options.
5. (n.) A union of people or countries joined in a pact or treaty for a shared goal.
8. (n.) A sudden realization or awakening of knowledge.
9. (n.) An industrial chemical used to make plastics that are often used in food and drink containers, that may cause various health problems including brain development troubles and high blood pressure.
12. (adj.) Awareness or knowledge of one's surroundings or of something. To do things intentionally.
14. (n.) A special assignment or chosen cause.
15. (adj.) An item that can be thrown away after one use.
16. (adj.) Thrown away.
17. (adj.) A container that may be used again, usually for liquids, such as shampoo.

Down
1. (n.) Large white bird of the southern hemisphere with long narrow wings.
4. (n.) Consciousness, cognizance. To have knowledge of.
6. (adj.) Absolutely necessary.
7. (v.) To stress as important.
10. (v.) To travel on water. To steer a vehicle. To carefully avoid troubles on a difficult path.
11. (v.) Past Participle. To hug. Take up a cause or an idea as one's own.
13. (adj.) Any object that may be used more than once.

B: Discussion Questions

1. Are you aware of the plastic pollution problem?
2. When did you first become aware?
3. How many plastic items do you have on you now?
4. How much plastic garbage does your house put out each week?(1 big bag?)
5. Do you think you can reduce that garbage?
6. Do you, or does anyone in your group, bring their own bag to the store or use a thermos instead of a pet bottle?

C: Research Activities

Look at the graphs below:
1. How many billion tons of plastic have we added to the world since 1950?

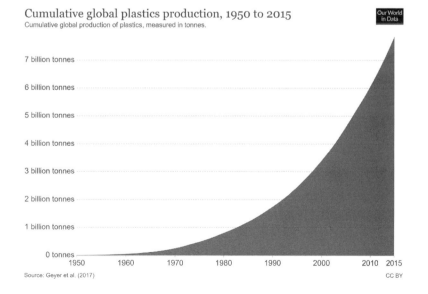

Cumulative global plastics production, 1950 to 2015
Cumulative global production of plastics, measured in tonnes.

Source: Geyer et al. (2017)   CC BY

2. Which region creates the most plastic pollution? Which region the least?

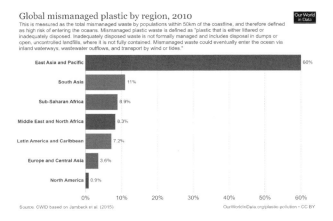

Global mismanaged plastic by region, 2010
This is measured as the total mismanaged waste by populations within 50km of the coastline, and therefore defined as high risk of entering the oceans. Mismanaged plastic waste is defined as "plastic that is either littered or inadequately disposed. Inadequately disposed waste is not formally managed and includes disposal in dumps or open, uncontrolled landfills, where it is not fully contained. Mismanaged waste could eventually enter the ocean via inland waterways, wastewater outflows, and transport by wind or tides."

Source: OWID based on Jambeck et al (2015)   OurWorldInData.org/plastic-pollution • CC BY

3. Which sector of industry creates the most plastic waste?

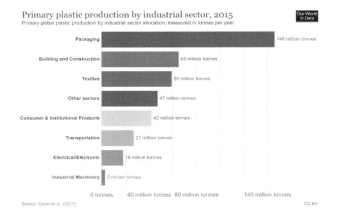

Primary plastic production by industrial sector, 2015
Primary global plastic production by industrial sector allocation, measured in tonnes per year.

Source: Geyer et al. (2017)   CC BY

1 **epiphany** 「悟りの瞬間」	
5 **Stouffer's** 冷凍加工食品で有名な食品メーカー.	
5 **Clif energy bar** 「クリフのエネルギーバー」エネルギー補助食品.	
6 **plastic tub** 「プラスティック容器」	
7 **shampoo bar** 「固形シャンプー」	
9 **apple cider vinegar** 「リンゴ酢」	
11 **baking soda** 「重曹」	

For Beth Terry, the epiphany came when she read an article about how albatross chicks are being killed by discarded plastics. It was time to banish plastic from her life.

First, she focused on her kitchen and got rid of the shopping bags, microwaveable Stouffer's macaroni and cheese, Clif energy bars and the prewashed salads in plastic tubs.

Then she turned to her bathroom, where she switched to shampoo bars instead of bottles and made her own hair conditioner from apple cider vinegar. Toothpaste without plastic packaging was exceptionally hard to find, so she started making her own with baking soda.

Sometimes her personal war on plastic created awkward moments. During a vacation to Disneyland in California, Ms. Terry and her husband left their reusable cloth bags in the hotel, soon discovering that the local supermarket only had plastic bags. How to carry a bunch of apples, oranges, avocados and melons?

"We just rolled it up in our T-shirts and carried it that way," said Ms. Terry, 54, recalling how she crab-walked back to the hotel to stay true to her principles. "If I let myself off the hook this time, it would be easier for me to take plastic next time."

Treating plastic like a drug habit that needs to be kicked is a lifestyle pledge being shared by more and more consumers, horrified by the tens of millions of metric tons of plastic created worldwide each year, much of it in the form of single-use items like straws, that end up in landfills or, worse, the oceans.

Stores that pride themselves on zero plastics have opened in New York and London, selling items like silicone water bottles, cardboard poop scoopers and iPhone cases made of flax.

Designers have embraced "plastic free" as a new challenge, whether it's building a supermarket aisle without plastics or making eco-friendly clothing that does not involve "virgin" plastics.

Some companies, like Procter & Gamble and PepsiCo will soon test selling products like Tropicana orange juice in glass bottles, Pantene shampoo in aluminum bottles and other items in refillable nonplastic containers, harking back to the days of the milkman.

"The awareness has exploded," said Susan Freinkel, a journalist in the Bay Area and the author of "Plastic: A Toxic Love Story." "The movement to get rid of trivial plastic has taken off. There is a critical mass of consciousness."

But to exist in the modern world without plastic, however noble a goal, may not actually be possible.

Grind Your Own

If you gathered up all your plastic waste each week, as Ms. Terry once did, you would have a huge mound on the floor. Where to even begin?

"The one thing I try to emphasize to people is to go step by step," said Ms. Terry, an accountant who lives in Greenbelt, Md., and who is the author of "Plastic-Free: How I Kicked the Plastic Habit and How You Can Too." "Don't try to do everything at once. It's been a practice of mine to not get overwhelmed by it all."

Once you wake up to the plastic problem, you see it everywhere: in jars of peanut butter and bags of grapes, in tubes of toothpaste and Tupperware containers, in bottles of Dawn dish soap and Tide laundry detergent, in the wrappers of Doritos chips and the lining of milk cartons.

To navigate the consumer minefield, plastic purgers find places where they can shop. It may take months, but they learn where to get milk in a glass bottle, or which store lets you grind your own peanut butter. And rather than see it as a huge inconvenience, they treat living plastic free as a fun game.

"I wake up and think, 'How am I going to make it through the day without using any single-use plastic?'" said Dianna Cohen, 53, an artist in Santa Monica, Calif., and a founder of Plastic Pollution Coalition, an advocacy group. "Right away the challenge hits you in the bathroom with the toothbrush."

For her, the answer is often the farmers' markets, which exist year-round in Southern California. Needless to say, she brings her own bags. "I'm a big fan of baskets," Ms. Cohen said. "I bring baskets and canvas bags to put vegetables in.

Like many who aim to live plastic free, Ms. Cohen never leaves home without her eco-survival kit, which includes a steel cup, a set of bamboo utensils, two stainless-steel straws and a cloth bag.

Plastic purgers need to rearrange their lives to avoid the offending material. If a restaurant serves food only on plastic plates, they won't eat there. Fast food? Most wrappers contain plastic. Smoothies from a juice bar? Unless they put the smoothie in a stainless-steel to-go cup, move on, or make your own at home. Bread? Buy it from a local bakery to avoid fresh-seal bags.

But there are certain situations where plastics are unavoidable. Try having a medical procedure without using a plastic syringe or an intravenous drip bag. Plastic water bottles can be indispensable after natural disasters.

Despite their best efforts, the purgers all say they can't totally banish plastic from their lives. For Ms. Cohen, it's a favorite hairbrush she has had for decades. And Ms. Terry confronts the limits of her plastic ban each time she visits the pharmacy, where no pharmacist would put medicine in a Mason jar. "It's a daily challenge," Ms. Cohen said.

Pig-Hair Toothbrushes

Going plastic free is also easier these days because there's more awareness and alternatives. Stores now sell dental floss made of silk, wooden toothbrushes with pig-hair bristles, stainless-steel ice cube trays, food wrappers made with beeswax coated cotton, and other nonplastic versions of household items.

Jay Sinha and Chantal Plamondon, who live in Wakefield, Quebec, started the store Life Without Plastic in 2006, a few years after their son was born. They wanted to avoid exposing him to bisphenol A, found in many baby bottles, but they had trouble finding a safer alternative. When Ms. Plamondon tracked down a glass bottle, it was one of the first items they sold.

"It was more the mother crowd before, but in the past few years, it's about plastic pollution, the oceans," Ms. Plamondon said. "Recently we noticed more millennials shopping the site."

One of those younger converts is Tessa Carleton, 24, who makes and sells handmade goods like macramé in rural Quebec. After a conversation with an environmentalist friend four years ago, Ms. Carleton donated or gave away the shampoo bottles, nail polish remover and Ziploc bags.

The farmhouse she shares with her husband, Jacob, feels like a 75-year-old time capsule. In addition to raising pigs and chickens for food, they make their own deodorant, lip balm and body moisturizer. It's domestic life before the Plastic Age.

Still, some wonder whether buying metal ice-cube trays is just another example of conscious consumerism. Buying a four-pack of metal straws at Urban Outfitters can be a kind of trendy virtue signaling. It offers a way to feel good without examining one's larger environmental impact (like the energy required to ship glass or metal, both heavier than plastic).

But those committed to living plastic free say that the small steps add up and make an impact. "Given that single-use disposable plastics are at the heart of the plastic pollution problem, if you do these simple things, you could potentially reduce your plastic consumption by 80 percent or maybe even more," said Mr. Sinha, who wrote a guide to avoiding plastics with Ms. Plamondon.

Nevertheless, it is usually more expensive to buy stainless-steel or wood items instead of plastic ones, or fresh foods instead of packaged ones. And it can be difficult to avoid plastic in poorer communities. Not everyone has access to year-round farmers' markets, or the means to shop at them.

Kristal Ambrose, 29, an environmental scientist who founded the Bahamas Plastic Movement, an advocacy group, faces that challenge daily. Much of what is sold on the island nation is imported and shipped in plastic.

---

5 **bisphenol A** 「ビスフェノール A」
baby bottle 「哺乳瓶」
6 **track down** 「やっと見つける」
8 **mother crowd** 「母親たちの集まり」
10 **millennials** 「ミレニアル世代」主に 1981～1996 生まれの人をさす.

18 **deodorant** 「制汗剤」

21 **conscious consumerism** 「意識の高い消費行動」→ Note 1
22 **Urban Outfitters** 衣服, 雑貨, 家具などを扱うアメリカのメーカー.
virtue signaling → Note 2
24 **ship** 「輸送する」
26 **committed to ~** 「～に本気で取り組んでいる」
27 **given that ~** 「～を考慮すると」

"I avoid plastic in areas where I can control," said Ms. Ambrose, who carries bamboo cutlery and a reusable bottle with her at all times. "For me, not using a plastic bag means so much more. But the mother who's juggling work, kids, other things — their priorities are different."

Part of her mission is to show that you don't need to be rich to avoid plastic. "Sometimes people can't afford a bamboo kit, but you can take a fork from home," Ms. Ambrose said. "Even an old pasta sauce jar can be made into a reusable item."

Notes

1　conscious consumerism とは環境や人権を意識した消費行動のこと. 物を買う時私たちは中身と値段のバランスを見て買うかどうか決めるが, conscious consumerism ではその商品が環境にやさしいかどうか, 製造過程でその商品にかかわった労働者の人権が尊重されているかなどを意識して, 値段よりも倫理的に正しい商品かどうかが購入の決め手となる. 意識を高く保つためには正しい教育と時間が必要で, 商品も通常より高いことが多いため, 一部では, お金と時間のある人たちだけの贅沢な消費行動だという批判もある.

2　virtue signaling とは, 他の人より道徳的に正しい行動をとっていることを強調したり, 正しい政治的観念を持っていることを誇示することをいう.

Post-reading

A: Word Match

Match the compounds to their description

1. Drug habit		a. People who wish to remove all petroleum based products from their lives.
2. Virgin plastics		b. The minimum amount of people aware of a problem needed in order to change it.
3. Off the hook		c. Items that cause problems, in this case plastic.
4. Critical mass of consciousness		d. New, never used petroleum based products.
5. Consumer minefield		e. One's way of existence at home.
6. Plastic purgers		f. Dangerous shopping traps. In this case the difficulties of not buying plastic goods.
7. Advocacy group		g. A container full of objects from an earlier era.
8. Offending materials		h. Buying products with specific intentions.
9. Time capsule		i. The daily use of illegal substances, here used as a comparison to our addiction to plastic.
10. Domestic life		j. The effect on nature.
11. Conscious consumerism		k. A coalition of people actively supporting a cause.
12. Environmental impact		l. Go unpunished. Not have to face consequences.

B: Comprehension Questions

1. What caused Beth Terry's epiphany?
2. How did she banish plastic from her bathroom?
3. What life style pledge are more and more consumers making?
4. What products will companies like Procter & Gamble and PepsiCo soon test?
5. What does Ms. Terry emphasize people do to kick the plastic habit?
6. How do plastic purgers treat living plastic-free?
7. What does Ms. Cohen's "eco-survival kit" include?
8. In which situations are plastics unavoidable?
9. What kind of alternatives exist to plastic products these days?
10. Why did Jay Sinha and Chantal Plamondon start their store Life Without Plastic?
11. What is at the heart of the plastic pollution problem?
12. What is Ms. Ambrose's mission?

C: Discussion Questions

1. After reading the article has anything shocked you about the amount of plastic waste in the world?
2. Rethink about the plastic you use at home. What could you stop using?
3. What other kinds of things might you stop using or change in order to use less plastic?
4. Have you heard of natural food stores, or bring your own container stores? If not what do you think they are and where can they be found?
5. Do you think Japan's tradition of wrapping everything up can be changed?

D: Research Questions

1. What is the size of the plastic garbage island in the middle of the Pacific Ocean?
2. Where does most of the garbage in the Pacific Ocean come from?
3. What percentage of this garbage comes from your country?
4. Make a list with two columns of products from your kitchen that you can change to avoid using plastic. In one column write down the plastic product, in the second column write down the alternative.
   Plastic product: Alternative:
5. Make a similar list with two columns for products from your bathroom.
   Plastic product: Alternative:
6. What is plastic made out of?
7. What does plastic become when it breaks down?
8. What alternative materials are now being researched to use instead of plastic?

Unit 2
Rwanda Is Winning War on Plastic Bags

By Kimiko de Freytas-Tamura   Oct. 28, 2017

Pre-reading

A: Crossword

Match the words in the Word Bank to their descriptions to fill in the crossword.

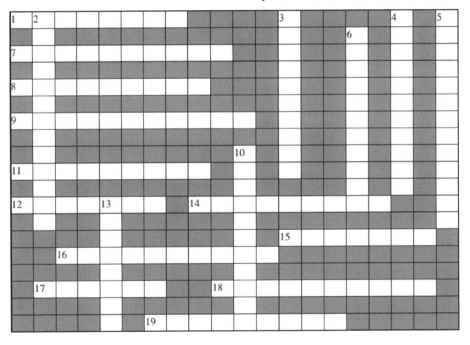

Word Bank

Authoritarian	Bashfully	Biodegradable	Broadcast	Cellophane	Clogging
Compromises	Confessions	Contraband	Enforcement	Illicit	Imprisoned
Jabbing	Nefarious	Negotiate	Obedient	Policy	Traffickers
Vigilantes					

Across

1. (adj.) Willfully following the laws, rules or instructions of those in authority.
7. (n.) Goods that are forbidden to be imported or exported by law.
8. (adj.) Extremely bad or evil.
9. (n.) Marketers or sellers of goods for money — usually refers to illegal goods.
11. (adv.) Shyly, or timidly.
12. (adj.) Forbidden by law, or contrary to accepted morality.
14. (v.) To spread or send over a wide area, transmit by radio waves.
15. (v.) Present participle. To stab, poke, or pierce.
16. (n.) People who take the law into their own hands and attack people they believe are guilty of breaking the law.
17. (n.) A plan of action set by an individual group or government.
18. (n.) A paper thin sheet of plastic used to wrap food to keep it fresh and dry.
19. (v.) To talk terms to come to an agreement.

Down

2. (adj.) Materials capable of being broken down by nature.
3. (v.) Past participle. To be put in jail, locked up.
4. (n.) Written or spoken admissions of crimes, misdeeds or faults.
5. (adj.) Characteristic of absolute rule. The dictatorial demanding of unquestioning obedience.
6. (v.) Agree to a middle way between two sides, or in this case, to weaken a position.
10. (n.) The act of making sure people follow the law.
13. (v.) Present participle. To block the flow of something, like water. Back up, choke, congest.

B: Discussion Questions

1. How many plastic bags do you use a week?
2. How about in your house?
3. Do you, or either of your parents, bring your own bag when you shop?
4. Do you, or any one in your group, work in a store that uses lots of bags?
5. Have you ever witnessed, or seen on T.V. or internet, some of the plastic pollution?
6. What do you think of making plastic bags illegal?

C: Research Activities

Look at the map:

1. Write in the name of the continent, which Rwanda is a part of.
2. Write in the names of the 4 countries bordering Rwanda.
3. Write in the name of the 2 major lakes in the region.
4. Write in the name of the capital of Rwanda.
5. Write the names of two rivers in Rwanda on the lines below.

_____

_____

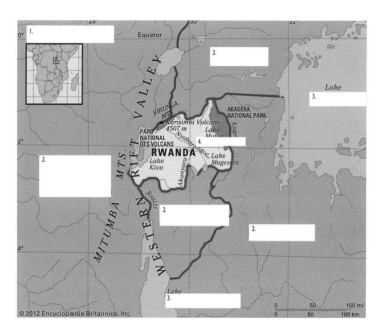

GISENYI, Rwanda — They are sometimes tucked into bras, hidden in underwear or coiled tightly around a smuggler's arms.

They're not narcotics or even the illegally mined gold and diamonds that frequently make it across the border into Rwanda. But they are, at least in the eyes of Egide Mberabagabo, a watchful border guard, every bit as nefarious.

The offending contraband? Plastic bags.

"They're as bad as drugs," said Mr. Mberabagabo, one of several border officials whose job is to catch smugglers and dispose of the illicit plastic.

In Rwanda, it is illegal to import, produce, use or sell plastic bags and plastic packaging except within specific industries like hospitals and pharmaceuticals. The nation is one of more than 40 that have banned, restricted or taxed the use of plastic bags, including China, France and Italy.

But Rwanda's approach is different. Traffickers caught carrying illegal plastic are liable to be fined, jailed or forced to make public confessions.

Smugglers can receive up to six months in jail. The executives of companies that keep or make illegal plastic bags can be imprisoned for up to a year, officials say. Stores have been shut down and fined for wrapping bread in cellophane, their owners required to sign apology letters — all as part of the nation's environmental cleanup.

Plastic bags, which take hundreds of years to degrade, are a major global issue, blamed for clogging oceans and killing marine life. In September, Kenya made a rule that will punish anyone making, selling or importing plastic bags with as much as four years in jail or a $19,000 fine.

In Rwanda, the authorities say the bags contribute to flooding and prevent crops from growing because rainwater can't penetrate the soil when it is littered with plastic.

The nation's zero tolerance policy toward plastic bags appears to be paying off: Streets in the capital, Kigali, and elsewhere across this hilly, densely populated country are virtually spotless. Men and women are regularly seen on the sides of roads sweeping up rubbish, and citizens are required once a month to partake in a giant neighborhood cleanup, including the president.

Plastic-bag vigilantes are everywhere, from airports to villages, and these informants tip off the authorities about sales or use of plastic.

One recent afternoon, Mr. Mberabagabo surveyed the crossing point with the Democratic Republic of Congo, where thousands of people, goods and animals flowed back and forth.

Plastic tubs filled with onions, eggplants, carrots, plantains and cassava bobbed above the heads of women who marched purposefully, with places to go, money to make and mouths to feed. And among them, often tucked in the women's undergarments, Mr. Mberabagabo said, were hundreds of plastic bags. "The most extreme cases are the ladies," he said. "It's not very easy to search them," he added bashfully.

An immigration official working alongside Mr. Mberabagabo showed footage on his cellphone of a middle-aged woman who had been caught transporting plastic bags wrapped around her arms. In the clip, she sobbed and apologized, shielding her eyes from the camera as if she were a drug dealer exposed in a sting operation on television.

Rwanda is probably Africa's cleanest nation. Though at least 15 African countries have enacted some sort of ban, many still have plastic bags littered on roads, stuck in drain pipes or caught in trees. Cattle die eating the bags because they obstruct digestion. In informal settlements in places like Kenya, plastic bags are sometimes used as "flying toilets" containing human waste.

There are, of course, many environmental threats on the

6 **bob** 「上下に揺れ動く」頭上に物を乗せて歩いているさま.

12 **immigration official** 「入国審査官」

13 **footage** 「ビデオ映像」

15 **clip** 「映像の一場面」

16 **sting operation** 「おとり捜査」

22 **informal settlement** 「スラム街」

23 **flying toilet** 「簡易トイレ」

Crossing into Gisenyi, Rwanda, from Congo. Border officials are on the lookout for smugglers trying to bring plastic bags into the country.   Diana Zeyneb Alhinfawi for The New York Times

写真：The New York Times/Redux/ アフロ

continent, including poaching, water pollution and deforestation. Some countries are trying to tackle them, like Gabon, where the president has fashioned himself as an environmentally conscious leader. But many nations lack the resources or political will. Congo bans plastic bags, in theory, but there is little to suggest the ban is enforced.

Kinshasa, Congo's capital, has so much trash, most of it contained in plastic bags, that the city's residents have nicknamed the city "poubelle," or "garbage can." In Goma, a Congolese city just across the border with Rwanda, plastic litter is everywhere, made even more visible because the earth there is made of black, volcanic rock. Clumps of colored plastic poke out of the ground like weird vegetation.

In Rwanda, enforcing the ban, which was first adopted in 2008, involves hundreds of rules that are tricky to follow.

Imports generally have their plastic packaging removed at customs, officials say, unless doing so would damage the goods. In that case, stores are required to remove the packaging before handing the merchandise to customers. Food wrapped in cellophane is allowed only in hotels, and only if it does not leave the premises.

Biodegradable bags are allowed only for frozen meat and fish, not for other items like fruit and vegetables because such bags still take as long as 24 months to decompose, the government says.

Potato chips and other foods packed in plastic are allowed only if the companies making them are approved by the government — after showing a detailed business plan that includes how they plan to collect and recycle their bags.

The results of Rwanda's efforts are evident in this clean country, but they may not be easy to replicate. In the United States and Europe, for example, there is a dispute between environmentalists and representatives of the plastics industry who say that bags made of alternative materials, like cloth, have a bigger carbon footprint than plastic ones and aren't as environmentally friendly as people think. Plastic bags should be reused and recycled instead, they argue.

The authorities in Rwanda brush off criticism about the absence of similar debates in their country. The rules here are based on extensive scientific research and public surveys, they say. And their enforcement is more easily accepted in a country with authoritarian tendencies and little room for dissent.

3　**environmentally conscious**　「環境意識が高い」

17　**customs**　「税関」

20　**premise**　「(ホテルの)敷地」

32　**carbon footprint**　「CO$_2$排出量」

36　**brush off**　「無視する」

---

1 **Paul Kagame**
「ポール・カガメ」
→ Note 1

2 **hammer ~ into**
shape 「苦心して
〜を作り上げる」

4 **the 1994 genocide**
→ Note 1

6 **Mr. Kagame's**
signature style
大統領の署名ひと
つで政策が決まる
トップダウン方式の
こと．

8 **thatched roof**
「藁葺き屋根」

11 **detention center**
「一時拘留所」

16 **pose as ~** 「〜のふ
りをする」

23 **jab one's finger at**
~ 「〜に指を突き
立てて責める」

26 **under one's breath**
「小声で」

32 **go bad** 「傷む」

Out of deep anxiety over national security, President Paul Kagame has hammered into shape an obedient, organized society of law-abiding and law-fearing citizens who have grown accustomed to a strong government after the 1994 genocide, in which nearly a million people were killed in 100 days. 5

Tough enforcement is Mr. Kagame's signature style, even when it comes to developing his country. He requires all Rwandans to wear shoes, has eradicated huts with thatched roofs and has banned imports of used clothing because he says it compromises dignity.

Children here are taught in schools not to use plastic bags and 10 to cherish the environment. Smugglers are often held in detention centers or forced to write confessions in newspapers or broadcast them on the radio. Supermarkets caught selling food in plastic packaging are shut down until they pay a fine and write an apology.

Two officials from Rwanda's Environment Management 15 Authority recently went on an inspection of shops in Kigali, posing as customers. By the end of the hour, they had already padlocked three stores and fined the owners a few hundred dollars each for selling bread wrapped in cellophane, using biodegradable bags for vegetables and cookies, or selling flour packaged in plastic instead 20 of paper.

"This is very bad," said Martine Uwera, one of the inspectors, towering over a store employee and jabbing her finger at a loaf of bread wrapped in plastic.

"Forgive us," the worker pleaded. "We didn't know, we didn't 25 know." A colleague muttered, "It's not fair," under her breath. The store was closed temporarily until the fine was paid and the owner signed an apology letter.

Another store in the vicinity was fined and lost revenue worth $650, a sizable amount here. Its owner, Emile Ndoli, a baker, tried 30 to negotiate with the inspectors and an argument erupted. Bread wrapped in paper, he said, went bad faster than bread wrapped in plastic.

"What Rwanda is doing is 100 percent correct," he said. "But I'm also a businessman and I want a permanent solution, which won't 35 involve losing money."

Notes

1 ルワンダでは多数派のフツ族と少数派のツチ族の対立が長年続いていたが，1994年，フツ族出身の大統領が乗った飛行機が何者かによって撃墜されたことをきっかけに対立が激化，100日ほどの間に数十万人のツチ族がフツ族によって命を奪われるという民族大虐殺が起こった．この状況の中，隣国ウガンダでツチ族によって組織されたルワンダ愛国戦線が巻き返しに成功してルワンダ全土を制圧した．ルワンダ愛国戦線の指揮を執ったのがアメリカで軍事訓練を受けたこともあるツチ族出身の軍人ポール・カガメ氏だった．彼は2000年に圧倒的な得票率で大統領となり，アフリカの奇跡とも呼ばれる経済成長を実現して近代化に成功した一方で，2034年まで大統領在任を可能にした憲法の改正をはじめ，その強引な政治手法は独裁的とも批判されている．

Post-reading

A: Word Match

Match the compounds to their description

1. Coiled tightly		a. Removal of pollution from nature.
2. Offending contraband		b. People's feces.
3. Public confessions		c. A secret action plan that tricks people into revealing their crimes.
4. Environmental cleanup		d. Wound closely.
5. Marine life		e. Habit of acting in a dictatorial manner.
6. Zero tolerance		f. Places where people are held while awaiting trial. Temporary confinement cells.
7. Sting Operation		g. Creatures of the sea.
8. Informal settlement		h. Following the rules.
9. Human waste		i. Bothersome illegal product.
10. Carbon footprint		j. An answer to a problem that lasts forever.
11. Authoritarian tendencies		k. Unofficial towns or living areas.
12. Law-abiding		l. Admission of guilt to society at large.
13. Detention centers		m. The amount of CO_2 a person leaves in nature.
14. Permanent solution		n. Absolutely no acceptance or allowance.

B: Comprehension Questions

1. What illegal goods are smugglers trying to bring into Rwanda and how are they hiding it?
2. What does Mr. Mberabagabo, a border guard, compare plastic bag to?
3. Specifically which industries only are allowed to use plastic products?
4. What other countries have banned, restricted or taxed the use of plastic bags?
5. How long can smugglers and executives of companies that make illegal products be imprisoned?
6. Why are countries banning plastic bags?
   (Use information from a few paragraphs: Hint Paragraphs 8, & 15)

7. Which is the cleanest country in Africa and why?
8. When are companies allowed to package food in plastic?
9. How do representatives of the plastic industry in the US argue for plastic?
10. Why has Rwanda been successful in enforcing the ban on plastic?
11. What encourages Rwandans to obediently accept the strong government?
12. What did the store owner Emile Ndoli, who was fined and lost $650 of revenue, say about the government shut down of stores over plastic use?

C: Discussion Questions

1. Given that Rwanda is now considered the cleanest country in Africa, do you think that their making plastic bags illegal is a good idea?
2. Do you think other countries should follow?
3. How about Japan? Should Japan make plastic bags and packaging illegal?
4. Do you bring your own bag when you shop?
5. What is the best way to stop people doing things?
6. Probably you are all law-abiding citizens, but what would you do if you suddenly had to give up something you use everyday and like using. For example, imagine if it became illegal to use petroleum based makeup (eyeliner's, lipsticks, nail polishes etc.) because of all its little containers etc.? Or what if the internet or smart phone apps became illegal? Discuss in your group how you would react. Would you obey the law? Or would you try to smuggle make up or smart phones etc.?
7. What are some alternatives to the products you had to give up in question 6?
8. What else do you know about Rwanda?

D: Research Questions

1. Name 5 more of the 40 countries that have banned plastic bags in some way.
2. Research some alternatives to plastic bags that are being used in other countries.
3. List some other ways that may discourage people from using plastic bags.
4. List some of the alternatives to using plastic bags and products.
5. Think of a few products that you think should be illegal but are now allowed. Why?
6. Choose one of those products and decide how you would get people to stop using it.
7. Who are the main ethnic groups in Rwanda? Why was there tension between them?
8. What event lead to the genocide and how did the United Nations react?

II

Industry Invades the Borders of Health

Unit 3

An Epidemic of Overweight Africans

By Jeffrey Gettleman   Jan. 27, 2018

Pre-reading

A: Crossword

Match the words in the Word Bank to their descriptions to fill in the crossword.

Word Bank

Affluent	Cardiologists	Deprived	Epidemic	Famine	Hypertension	Indulges
Jeers	Looming	Malnutrition	Metabolism	Nutrients	Obesity	Prone
Restricting	Sedentary	Stigma	Urbanization	Waistline		

Across

1. (n.) The organic processes necessary for life.
4. (adj.) Disadvantaged. Lacking in necessities.
6. (adj.) Having a tendency (e.g. to get sick.)
10. (n.) Heart specialists, heart surgeons.
11. (n.) A mark of disgrace associated with a person, quality or circumstance. Shame.
13. (n.) Any substance (food or chemical) that provides energy to animals to build tissues, or to plants for organic synthesis.
14. (v.) Gerund. To put a limit on something. Keep under control.
15. (n.) The measurement around a person's waist. The size of their stomach.
16. (adj.) Rich. Wealthy
17. (n.) An extreme lack of food.
18. (n.) The turning of a rural area into a city or town.

Down

1. (n.) A lack or excess in necessary nutrients due to a poor diet or inability to absorb foods.
2. (adj.) Involving sitting or doing next to no activity.
3. (n.) Rude, mocking remarks.
5. (n.) Abnormally high blood pressure.
7. (n.) A widespread outbreak of an infectious disease.
8. (v.) Present participle. To hang over, brood, appear in a threatening manner.
9. (n.) More than average overweight.
12. (v.) Allowing someone the pleasure of something desired. Satisfy.

B: Discussion Questions

1. Have you ever been on a diet?
2. What kind of diet do you think works best?
3. How much junk food do you eat per day/week?
4. Do you think the Japanese diet is changing?
5. Do you think your generation is as healthy as that of your parents or grandparents?

C: Research Activities

Look at the chart below:
1. How long ago did the obesity problem begin for most countries?
2. Is there any surprise in this chart for you?
3. Which are the 5 most obese countries on the graph?
4. Which of these countries has likely gotten thinner?

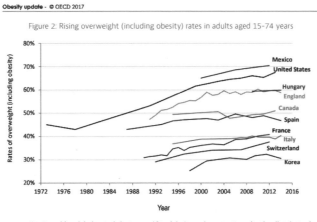

Look at the map on the next page:
5. What is the percentage rate of obesity in your country?

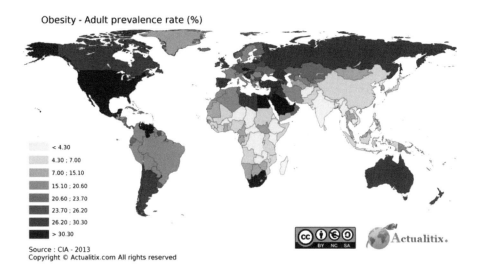

Obesity - Adult prevalence rate (%)

< 4.30
4.30 ; 7.00
7.00 ; 15.10
15.10 ; 20.60
20.60 ; 23.70
23.70 ; 26.20
26.20 ; 30.30
> 30.30

Source : CIA - 2013

NAIROBI, Kenya — As she walks through the alleyways of her poor neighborhood, Valentine Akinyi weathers the jeers yelled at her: "Elephant, elephant, elephant." She has gotten used to the insults, she said, but still, it hurts. "Who's going to want to marry me?" she asked.

It used to be difficult in Kenya to find many people built like Ms. Akinyi, who, at 5 feet 9 inches tall and 285 pounds, is obese.

In Africa, the world's poorest continent, malnutrition is stubbornly widespread and millions of people are desperately hungry, with famine conditions looming in some war-torn countries.

But in many places, growing economies have led to growing waistlines. Obesity rates in sub-Saharan Africa are shooting up faster than in just about anywhere else in the world, causing a public health crisis that is catching Africa, and the world, by surprise.

In Burkina Faso, the prevalence of adult obesity in the past 36 years has jumped nearly 1,400 percent. In Ghana, Togo, Ethiopia and Benin, it has increased by more than 500 percent. Eight of the 20 nations in the world with the fastest-rising rates of adult obesity are in Africa, according to a recent study at the University of Washington.

It is part of a seismic shift in Africa as rapid economic growth transforms every aspect of life, including the very shape of its people.

Many Africans are eating more junk food, much of it imported. They are also getting much less exercise, as millions of people abandon a more active farming life to crowd into cities, where they tend to be more sedentary. More affordable cars and a wave of motorbike imports also mean that fewer Africans walk to work.

6　**built like ~**　「～の
　　ような体格の」

12　**sub-Saharan
　　Africa**「サハラ以
　　南のアフリカ」→
　　Note 1
13　**just about = almost
　　catch ~ by surprise**
　　「～を驚かせる」
16　**prevalence**　「率,
　　割合」

Obesity may be a tough battle in Africa for other reasons. For one, people who did not get enough nutrients when they were young (which is still a problem in Africa) are more prone to putting on weight when lots of food is available. And second, African health systems are heavily geared toward combating other diseases. 5

African doctors say their public health systems have been so focused on AIDS, malaria, tuberculosis and tropical fevers — historically, Africa's big killers — that few resources are left for what are called noncommunicable diseases, like diabetes and heart ailments. 10

"What we are seeing is likely the worst epidemic the country will ever see, probably in the long run worse than the H.I.V. epidemic of the '90s," said Anders Barasa, a cardiologist in Kenya, referring to obesity and its related diseases. "But changing the health care system to cater for obesity related diseases is like turning a 15 supertanker."

In Kenya, one of Africa's most developed nations, there are around 40 cardiologists for the entire population of 48 million people. In the United States, there is one cardiologist for every 13,000 people. 20

Even as the obesity problem worsens, Africa's older problem of malnutrition has hardly vanished. While millions of Africans are eating unhealthy foods or overeating, millions of Africans are still starving or near to it. Last year was one of the worst on record for hunger. 25

Health professionals say that people who grow up deprived of nutrients, as millions of Africans do, run a higher risk of later becoming obese. During famine times, one of the body's defense mechanisms is to slow down metabolism to hold onto every calorie. When feast times come, metabolism often remains slow. Such 30 metabolic disorders can lead to all kinds of health problems later on, some of them life threatening.

One leading Kenyan endocrinologist, Nancy Kunyiha said that when she started a diabetes practice years ago, her medical school colleagues thought she was crazy. " 'There's no way you can 35 survive off diabetes,' " she said they warned her. " 'You got to do something else.' "

But Type II diabetes is closely linked to obesity, and sub-Saharan Africa is in the midst of a "rapidly expanding diabetes epidemic," a recent report found. In the past decade, Dr. Kunyiha's diabetes 40

6 **public health system** 「公的医療制度」
7 **tropical fevers** 「熱帯病」デング熱や狂犬病など．

13 **cardiologist** 「心臓病専門医」
14 **health care system** 「医療制度」
15 **cater for ~** 「~に応じる」

26 **deprived of ~** 「~が不足して」

30 **feast time** 「食料が豊かな時期」
31 **metabolic disorder** 「代謝異常」

33 **endocrinologist** 「内分泌内科医」
34 **diabetes practice** 「糖尿病の診療業務」
36 **survive off ~** 「~で食べていく」

practice has quadrupled, and most days her waiting room at the Aga Khan hospital in Nairobi, Kenya's capital, is standing room only.

Kenya's obesity rate, which is close to one in 10 people, is still far below industrialized countries like the United States (where more than one-third of adults are obese). But Kenya's rate is rising fast, more than doubling since 1990.

Now, many Kenyans are thinking about obesity for the first time. Ms. Akinyi says she reads articles in the local papers about obesity. But what the writers recommend to lose weight, she cannot afford.

She is a high school dropout, a single mother and a washerwoman; on about $40 a month, she supports herself and three children. Millions of Africans are just like her: trapped between the old and the new. They might not be destitute like their parents were. But they are still poor.

While they have just enough money to buy processed foods like potato chips, which are now widely available in low-income areas for a few cents, they often do not have enough to join a gym or buy fish or fresh vegetables.

And instead of working in the fields (which is how most Kenyans lived just a generation ago), they are marooned in squalid urban areas and are less physically active. Some of the least expensive foods to buy in the Kibera slum where Ms. Akinyi lives are French fries and fried dough, each around 20 cents. Apples, at the equivalent of 40 cents, are outside her budget, though soda isn't.

"And I love Sprite," Ms. Akinyi said with a guilty smile.

One of Coca-Cola's strategies in Kenya has been to reach the lower economic classes by making smaller 200 milliliter bottles that cost about 15 cents (compared with the standard 300 milliliter bottle that costs 25 cents). Burger King, Domino's, Cold Stone Creamery and Subway have all recently opened their first stores in Kenya, part of their strategy to break into Africa.

Despite insults like "elephant," there is also a stigma to being thin in some Kenyan circles. It goes back generations but was especially true in the 1990s, at the height of the AIDS epidemic when millions of Africans died. To many Kenyans, Dr. Kunyiha said, being thin still means being poor or sick. "It's really frustrating," Dr. Kunyiha said. "The image here is: The bigger your tummy, the better you're doing."

One of her patients, she says, is a rich man who drives a Mercedes and suffers from hypertension and obesity. She keeps

---

2 **standing room only** 「満席」

15 **processed food** 「加工食品」

23 **French fry** 「フライドポテト」
fried dough 「揚げパン」

31 **break into ~** 「~ に進出する」

Samuel, 13, center, the son of Fraciah Wangari, exercising during a physical education class at Muthaiga Primary School in Nairobi. He is teased about his weight.

Andrew Renneisen for The New York Times

写真：The New York Times/Redux/ アフロ

telling him to switch from fast food and meat to the old fashioned Kenya diet of beans, carrots and a vegetable called sukuma wiki that is similar to kale. "But he tells me he's come too far to eat like that because that's what he ate when he was a poor kid," she said.

Several Kenyan parents said they felt deeply conflicted about restricting their children's diet. Fraciah Wangari grew up in a poor village and does not want to deny her son. "I remember what it was like to really want biscuits but not be able to afford them," she said.

So she indulges her only child, Samuel, 13, who is obese, with a big belly. He's beginning to have circulation problems and says his joints hurt. Ms. Wangari recently splurged for a doctor's visit but many of the nutritious foods the doctor suggested, like fish, were way beyond her budget.

Affluent Kenyans have more options. It is not uncommon in Nairobi's fancier neighborhoods to see middle-aged men and women jogging their way up the hills, decked out in bright spandex. Just 10 years ago that was an unusual sight.

The Kenyan government, like other African governments, seems to have been slow to recognize the problem. The Health Ministry is still much more focused on promoting protected sex than good nutrition.

Africa is urbanizing faster than any other region of the world. In 1980, only 28 percent of Africans lived in urban areas. Today, that number is 40 percent, and by 2030, it is predicted to be 50 percent. The urbanization is driven partly by high birthrates and a shrinking availability of land, creating an exodus of millions of Africans from rural areas.

"If you're working in the field eight hours a day, you can eat anything you want," Dr. Barasa said. "But if you're sedentary, your requirements totally change."

10 **circulation problem** 「循環器の異常」

16 **decked out ~** 「～をカッコよく着て」
spandex 「スパンデックス製のスポーツウェア」伸縮性があり身体にフィットしたウェア.

19 **Health Ministry** 「保健省」

20 **protected sex** 「（性感染症予防のための）安全な性行為」

28 **your requirements** 「あなたに課されるもの」

Notes

1 sub-Saharan Africa とは，サハラ砂漠の南に位置するアフリカの国々，あるいは一帯をさす．北アフリカに比べると貧困率が高く，紛争や感染症，飢餓に苦しんできた地域である．しかし天然資源に恵まれ，インフラが整備されるなど，現在多くの国が急速な発展途上にあり，国によっては貧富の差が非常に大きくなっている．地理的にはサハラ砂漠以南のすべての地域をさす場合と，サハラ砂漠の南の端に沿った一帯をいう場合とがある．

Post-reading

A: Word Match

Match the compounds to their description

1. War-torn countries		a.	To adapt and provide for the needs of someone.
2. Growing economies		b.	An enormous change of direction or policy.
3. Seismic shift		c.	Strongly organized for obtaining a specific purpose.
4. Junk food		d.	Meals and snacks that are prepared in advanced with plenty of additives to make them last long.
5. Heavily geared		e.	Nations ravaged by conflict.
6. Non communicable diseases		f.	Illnesses not able to be transmitted from one person to another.
7. Turning a supertanker		g.	Quickly increasing finances.
8. Rapid economic growth		h.	An automatic reaction of the body against disease.
9. Cater for		i.	A disease in which the body develops high blood sugar levels, and a failure to respond to insulin.
10. Defense mechanisms		j.	Nations whose financial situation is increasing.
11. Type II diabetes		k.	City region.
12. Processed foods		l.	A person who quits secondary school
13. High school dropout		m.	Non-nutritious meals or snacks, usually processed.
14. Urban areas		n.	A metaphor for explaining how difficult it is to change the direction of a society by comparing it to a large ship.

B: Comprehension Questions

1. What do people jeer at Valentine Akinyi as she walks through the alleyways of her neighborhood?
2. What public health crisis is catching Africa and the world by surprise?
3. Why are people surprised?
4. By what percentage has the prevalence of adult obesity in Burkina Faso jumped in the past 36 years?
5. What are the main causes of this seismic shift? (Hint: Look at paragraphs 6 & 7.)
6. What are other reasons for Obesity?
7. Anders Barasa thinks obesity may be worse than what epidemic?
8. What does the body's defense mechanism do in times of famine and how does that

—28—

effect obesity?

9. What is Kenya's obesity rate?
10. Why do Kenyans buy processed foods?
11. Why is there a stigma to being thin in some Kenyans circles?
12. Why won't one of Dr. Kunyiha's patients eat the healthy traditional diet of beans, carrots, and sukuma wiki?

C: Discussion Questions

1. What is your image of Africa, Africans and African food? Would you ever go there?
2. What do you think of companies like Coca Cola and Burger King going into poor countries?
3. What is the longest you have gone without food?
4. Have you ever volunteered in a poor country? Would you like to?
5. What is similar between the seismic shift in the diet in Africa and in your country?
6. Do you know anyone with diabetes? Is it becoming a problem in Japan?
7. Are obese people stigmatized (made fun of) in your country? How?

D: Research Questions

1. List all the contributing reasons that obesity is now prevalent in Africa.
2. Look at the map below. List the names of 10 countries in Sub-Saharan Africa.
3. Look up 5 facts about Burkina Faso. Find its name on the map.
4. Research and describe the main traditional diet of Kenya or another African country.
5. What foods could you give up?
6. How many calories should a person eat each day?
7. How many calories does the average American eat? Kenyan eat? Japanese eat?

Source: GAO analysis of Department of State and USAID data (data); Map Resources (map). | GAO-15-300

Unit 4

West's Toxic E-Waste Despoils Thai Countryside

By Hannah Beech and Ryn Jirenuwat   Dec. 8, 2019

Pre-reading

A: Crossword

Match the words in the Word Bank to their descriptions to fill in the crossword.

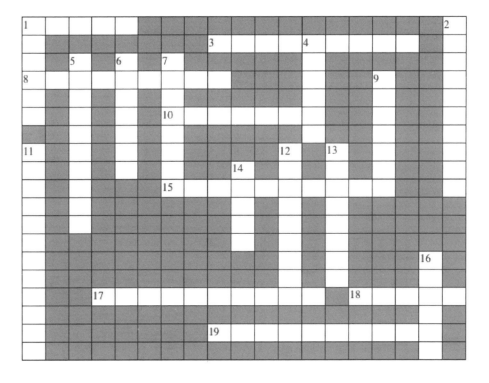

Word Bank

Accustomed	Castoff	Deluging	Dioxins	Fumes	Hoards	Implement
Incinerators	Infiltrate	Loopholes	Lucrative	Nauseating	Scrap	Spewed
Stockpiles	Tainted	Toiled	Toxic	Virtuous	Vulnerable	

Across

1. (adj.) Noxious, poisonous, harmful.
3. (n.) Ambiguities, especially in law, that make it possible to ignore or go around a law or a contract.
8. (adj.) Produces a big profit.
10. (v.) Past Participle. Corrupted, sullied, defiled, dirty, infected.
15. (n.) Reserves accumulated for future use. Backlog.
17. (v.) Pass through, enter, permeate.
18. (n.) Exhaust gases thrown out by an engine or chemicals.
19. (adj.) Easily hurt, or abused.

Down

1. (v.) Simple past. Worked very hard.
2. (v.) Present Participle. Sickening, revolting, disgusting.
4. (n.) Secret stashes. Lots of.
5. (adj.) Get used to, in the habit of.
6. (adj.) Thrown away, discarded.
7. (adj.) Morally excellent.
9. (n.) Toxic, cancer causing chemicals or gases that occur from burning plastics.
11. (n.) Furnaces for burning garbage.
12. (v.) Enforce, ensure, follow through (e.g. of laws).
13. (v.) Present Participle. Flooding. Overwhelming.
14. (n.) Rubbish, trash, worthless leftovers.
16. (v). Simple past. Spat out, vomited, threw up, ejected, sent out in large quantities.

B: Discussion Questions

1. How many smart phones, laptops or computers have you owned in your life?
2. What did you do with the old ones?
3. Where do you think they go? What happens to them?
4. Have you ever been to Thailand? Would you like to go?
5. What's your image of Thailand?

C: Research Activities

1. Fill in the names of the 4 countries bordering Thailand.

2. Fill in the names of the bodies of water surrounding Thailand.

3. Fill in the name of the capital of Thailand.

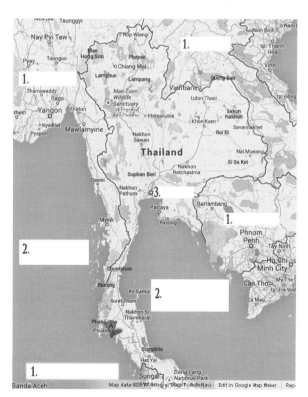

Look at the chart below and answer the questions:

4. Which continents are sending e-waste?
5. Which continents are receiving e-waste?

KOH KHANUN, Thailand — Crouched on the ground in a dimly lit factory, the women picked through the discarded innards of the modern world: batteries, circuit boards and bundles of wires.

They broke down the scrap — known as e-waste — with hammers and raw hands. Men, some with faces wrapped in rags to repel the fumes, shoveled the refuse into a clanking machine that salvages usable metal.

As they toiled, smoke spewed over nearby villages and farms. Residents have no idea what is in the smoke: plastic, metal, who knows? All they know is that it stinks and they feel sick.

The factory, New Sky Metal, is part of a thriving e-waste industry across Southeast Asia, born of China's decision to stop accepting the world's electronic refuse, which was poisoning its land and people. Thailand has become a center of the industry even as activists push back and its government wrestles to balance competing interests of public safety with the profits to be made from the lucrative trade.

Last year, Thailand banned the import of foreign e-waste. Yet new factories are opening across the country, and tons of e-waste are being processed, environmental monitors and industry experts say.

"E-waste has to go somewhere," said Jim Puckett, the executive director of the Basel Action Network, which campaigns against trash dumping in poor countries, "and the Chinese are simply moving their entire operations to Southeast Asia."

"The only way to make money is to get huge volume with cheap, illegal labor and pollute the hell out of the environment," he added.

Each year, 50 million tons of electronic waste are produced globally, according to the United Nations, as consumers grow accustomed to throwing away last year's model and acquiring the next new thing.

The notion of recycling these gadgets sounds virtuous: an infinite loop of technological utility. But it is dirty and dangerous work to extract the tiny quantities of precious metals — like gold, silver and copper — from castoff phones, computers and televisions.

For years, China took in much of the world's electronic refuse.

5

10

15

20

4 **environmental monitor** 「環境監視をする人」環境保護団体のメンバーなどのこと.
7 **the Basel Action Network** → Note 1

11 **the hell out of** 「徹底的に，滅茶苦茶に」

16 **gadget** 「電子機器」

Foreign workers sorting through piles of shredded e-waste on the premises of New Sky Metal in Thailand in September
Bryan Denton for The New York Times

写真：The New York Times/Redux/ アフロ

—33—

1	**Beijing**	「中国政府」
4	**cozy**	「癒着した」
9	**watchdog**	「監視機関」
11	**individual shipment**	「個人輸送の積荷」自治体などからの輸送貨物でないもの.
14	**the Thai Ministry of Industry**	「タイ工業省」
15	**with great fanfare**	「鳴り物入りで」
16	**raid**	「強制捜査」
19	**Laem Chabang Port customs bureau**	「レム・チャバン港税関」
26	**Chachoengsao**	「チャチュンサオ県」
34	**this long**	「こんなに長く」
35	**be outpaced by ~**	「～を下回っている」
38	**deputy director general**	「事務局次長」
39	**the Department of Industrial Works**	「タイ工場局」
	falsified declaration	「嘘の宣言」

Then in 2018, Beijing closed its borders to foreign e-waste. Thailand and other countries in Southeast Asia — with their lax enforcement of environmental laws, easily exploited labor force and cozy nexus between business and government — saw an opportunity.

"Every circuit and every cable is very lucrative, especially if there is no concern for the environment or for workers," said Penchom Saetang, the head of Ecological Alert and Recovery Thailand, an environmental watchdog.

While Southeast Asian nations like Indonesia, Malaysia and the Philippines have rejected individual shipments of waste from Western countries, Thailand was the first to push back more systematically against the electronic refuse deluging its ports.

In June of last year, the Thai Ministry of Industry announced with great fanfare the ban on foreign e-waste. The police made a series of high-profile raids on at least 10 factories, including New Sky Metal.

"New Sky is closed now, totally closed," Yutthana Poolpipat, the head of the Laem Chabang Port customs bureau, said in September. "There is no electronic waste coming into Thailand, zero."

But a recent visit to the hamlet of Koh Khanun showed that the factory was still running, as are many others, a reflection of the weak regulatory system and corruption that has tainted the country.

Since the e-waste ban, 28 new recycling factories, most dealing with electronic refuse, began operations in one province east of Bangkok, Chachoengsao, where Koh Khanun is located. This year, 14 businesses in that province were granted licenses to process electronic waste. Most of the new factories are in central Thailand between Bangkok and Laem Chabang, the nation's biggest port.

Thai officials say that factories are burning old stockpiles. Plants may also be processing domestic rather than foreign refuse, they say.

But neither explanation is likely, according to industry experts. Hoards of imported waste wouldn't last this long. And the amount of electronic trash that Thailand produces is far outpaced by the number of new factories.

Foreign e-waste might be smuggled into the country mislabeled as scrap, said Banjong Sukreeta, the deputy director general of the Department of Industrial Works. "Ask customs about falsified declarations," he said. "Rules are not enough if the people who

—34—

implement them are not up to it."

But Mr. Yutthana, of the customs bureau, said every box that landed at his port was inspected thoroughly. "We are 100 percent careful," he said.

5 **loosened** 「緩和された」
8 **pollution monitoring** 「汚染物質の定期測定」
9 **draft bill** 「法案」

In October of this year, the Thai legislature unveiled loosened labor and environmental regulations for all factories, a move that has benefited the e-waste industry. Under one provision, small companies are no longer subject to pollution monitoring. At the same time, a draft bill that would ensure tighter control over Thailand's electronic waste industry has languished.

"Thailand is welcoming environmental degradation with its own laws," said Somnuck Jongmeewasin, a lecturer in environmental management at Silpakorn University International College. "There are so many loopholes and ways to escape punishment."

The consequences are frightening. If some types of electronic waste aren't incinerated at a high enough temperature, dioxins, which can cause cancer, infiltrate the food supply. Toxic heavy metals seep into the soil and groundwater.

"Why don't you in the West recycle your own waste?" said Phayao Jaroonwong, a farmer east of Bangkok, who said her crops had withered after an electronic waste factory moved in next door. "Thailand can't take it anymore," she said. "We shouldn't be the world's dumping ground."

Phra Chayaphat Kuntaweera, a Buddhist abbot, has watched as several waste-processing factories opened around his temple. Two more are under construction.

First, the monks began to cough, he said. Then they vomited. When the incinerators burned, their headaches raged. "Monks are people, too," he said. "We get sick from the fumes just like anyone else."

Next to New Sky Metal, Metta Maihala surveyed her eucalyptus plantation. The lake that waters the farm has clouded over, and the smell is nauseating.

Suddenly, through the rows of trees, a pair of Burmese workers emerged. The man showed burns on his arms from his work at New Sky Metal but said he had no idea what liquid had caused his wounds. The woman, Ei Thazin, said she received $10 a day for sorting metal. "I didn't know this was dangerous work," she said.

In Thailand, millions of undocumented workers from poorer countries like Myanmar and Cambodia are vulnerable to abuse, environmental watchdogs say, adding that the need for such laborers will only intensify.

"We can't choose the air we breathe," said Ms. Metta, the eucalyptus farmer. "Now there will be even more factories. We are all going to die a slow death. ⁵

Notes

1　the Basel Action Network は有毒廃棄物の国外移送を監視するアメリカの NGO 団体．1989 年に有毒廃棄物の国境を越える移動や処分を規制するバーゼル条約が採択された後，条約にちなんだ名前で設立され，今日まで活動している．

Post-reading

A: Word Match

Match the compounds to their description

1. Toxic fumes		a. Rival concerns.
2. Circuit board		b. Poisonous exhaust gases.
3. Competing interests		c. Workers who are able to be taken advantage of without fear of punishment.
4. Lucrative trade		d. Minerals of extremely high value, especially for the computer industry.
5. Infinite loop		e. Very public position.
6. Precious metals		f. The destruction of nature.
7. Lax enforcement		g. An endless cycle.
8. Easily exploited labor		h. Defender, protector of nature.
9. Environmental watchdog		i. A combination of rules and agencies that set limits and rules on businesses.
10. High profile.		j. A plug-in card for computers to increase its capabilities.
11. Regulatory system.		k. Weak or non-application of laws.
12. Falsified Declarations.		l. Surveillance of waste products from businesses.
13. Environmental degradation		m. Made up or faked public statements.
14. Pollution monitoring.		n. Buying and selling of goods with a big profit margin.

B: Comprehension Questions

1. Why has Thailand become the center of the e-waste industry?
2. What are the competing interests in Thailand regarding e-waste?
3. What is the only way to make money from e-waste?
4. How many tons of electronic waste are produced globally each year according to the United Nations?
5. Why is recycling electronic gadgets not virtuous?

6. When did China close it's border to foreign e-waste?
7. What did the Thai Ministry of Industry announce with great fanfare in June last year?
8. Why is that factory still running, as shown in a recent visit to Koh Khanun?
9. Why is Thailand welcoming environmental degradation, according to Somnuck Jongmeewasin?
10. What are the health consequences of burning e-waste at low temperatures?
11. What did farmer Phayao Jaroonwong ask of westerners?
12. How much money do Burmese workers get for doing this dangerous work?

C: Discussion Questions

1. What do you think of electronic waste after reading the article?
2. Do you think it is fair or good for rich countries like Canada and Japan to send their garbage to poorer countries like China, Philippines and Thailand?
3. What are some solutions to e-waste? What should we do about it?
4. Does Japan have good environmental protection laws?
5. Does Japan have a good environmental record in the world?
6. What's your image of Thailand before and after reading the article?
7. What are the similarities and differences of Thailand and Japan?
8. Discuss various foods and culture of Thailand.

D: Research Questions

1. How many electronic gadgets (computers, tablets, smart phones) will the average Japanese use in a lifetime?
2. How many tons of e-waste does your country produce each year?
3. What does your country do with the waste?
4. What are some of the precious metals used in electronic gadgets? Make a list.
5. Which countries do these metals mostly come from?
6. Which country has the highest amount of dioxins in the world?
7. What are some of the effects of dioxin?
8. Make a list of some of the similarities and differences of Thailand and Japan?

III

High Tech Overreaches the Realm of Education

Unit 5
College Cheating, A Global Business

By Farah Stockman and Carlos Mureithi   Sept. 7, 2019

Pre-reading

A: Crossword

Match the words in the Word Bank to their descriptions to fill in the crossword.

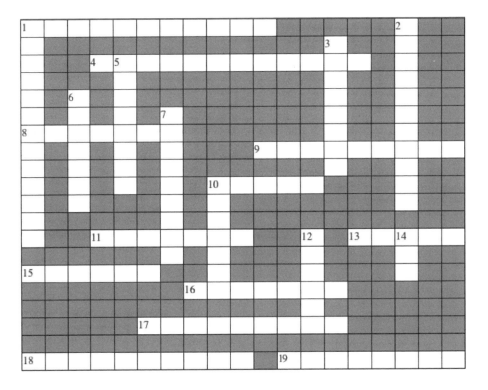

Word Bank

Ace	Blatant	Bribery	Confront	Detect	Desperate	Fraud
Flagged	Ghostwritten	Hotlines	Integrity	Metadata	Outsourcing	Plagiarism
Scandal	Scheme	Scrutinized	Sleek	Sophisticated	Tuition	Unethical

Across

1. (v.) Past participle. Inspected closely.
4. (adj.) A book or essay written for someone else who claims authorship.
8. (n.) The fee charged by a school to take classes.
9. (adj.) Not morally correct.
10. (adj.) Smooth and glossy. Elegant design.
11. (adj.) Obvious. Done openly and without shame.
13. (n.) Criminal deception of others for financial or personal gain.
15. (n.) A systematic plan to obtain an end. A secret plot.
16. (v.) Past participle. Marked for attention. Signaled.
17. (adj.) A feeling or situation of extreme need.
18. (n.) The act of using someone else's work and pretending it is your own.
19. (v.) To face someone or a problem head on. To bring up an issue face to face.

Down

1. (adj.) A person with a high degree of world experience and knowledge. A machine or object with a high degree of complexity.
2. (v.) Gerund. Contract work. Getting work done by someone else.
3. (n.) Information that gives knowledge about other information.
5. (n.) Direct telephone links for emergencies, usually for governments.
6. (n.) The giving or offering of a sum of money or other inducements to receive a favor.
7. (n.) The quality of having strong moral principles. Honesty.
10. (n.) A morally or illegally wrong action that causes public outrage.
12. (v.) Discover, find out, identify, uncover.
14. (v.) Informal. To do something perfectly.

B: Discussion Questions

1. Do you know what plagiarism is? Explain to your group.
2. Do you think it is bad? Why?
3. Have you ever cheated on an essay or test in school? How?
4. Did you get caught? What happened?
5. Were you aware of paid essay websites?
6. Have you ever considered using one?

C: Research Activities

1. Look at the African map to the right: Find Kenya and write its name.

2. Color red all the borders of the countries that were English colonies at one point.

3. Color blue all the borders of the countries that speak English now that are not already colored red.

4. Read the graph below. Which of the opinions do you agree with? Why?
   Discuss with partners.

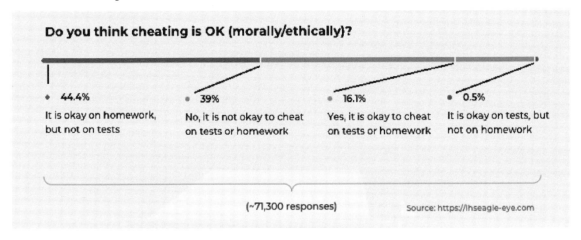

Do you think cheating is OK (morally/ethically)?

44.4%	39%	16.1%	0.5%
It is okay on homework, but not on tests	No, it is not okay to cheat on tests or homework	Yes, it is okay to cheat on tests or homework	It is okay on tests, but not on homework

(~71,300 responses)

Source: https://lhseagle-eye.com

Title **cheating** 「不正行為」
1 **due** 「支払い期日が来ている」
3 **selling insurance policy** 「保険のセールス」
5 **break into ~** 「~に参入する」
6 **industry** 「商売, 仕事」

Tuition was due. The rent was, too. So Mary Mbugua, a university student in Nyeri, Kenya, went out in search of a job. At first, she tried selling insurance policies. Then she sat behind the reception desk at a hotel, but it ran into financial trouble.

Finally, a friend offered to help her break into "academic writing," a lucrative industry in Kenya that involves doing school assignments online for college students in the United States, Britain and Australia. Ms. Mbugua felt conflicted. "This is cheating," she said. "But do you have a choice? We have to make money. We have to make a living."

11 **federal prosecutor** 「連邦検事」
federal prosecutors in the United States … → Note 1
13 **enjoy** 「(特権などを) 享受する」

Since federal prosecutors in the United States charged a group of rich parents and coaches this year in a sprawling fraud and bribery scheme, the advantages that wealthy American students enjoy in college admissions have been scrutinized. Less attention has been paid to the tricks some well-off students use once they are enrolled.

Cheating in college is nothing new, but the internet now makes it possible on a global, industrial scale. Sleek websites — with names like Ace-MyHomework and EssayShark — have sprung up

19 **bid on** 「入札する」

that allow people in developing countries to bid on and complete American homework assignments.

Although such businesses have existed for more than a decade, experts say demand has grown in recent years as the sites have become more sophisticated, with customer service hotlines and

24 **money-back guarantee** 「返金保証」
27 **essay-for-hire industry** 「レポート代行業」

money-back guarantees. The result? Millions of essays ordered annually in a vast, worldwide industry that provides enough income for some writers to make it a full-time job.

The essay-for-hire industry has expanded significantly in

developing countries with many English speakers, fast internet connections and more college graduates than jobs, especially Kenya, India and Ukraine. A Facebook group for academic writers in Kenya has over 50,000 members.

After a month of training, Ms. Mbugua began producing essays about everything from whether humans should colonize space ("it is not worth the struggle," she wrote) to euthanasia (it amounts to taking "the place of God," she wrote). During her best month, she earned $320, more money than she had ever made in her life.

A 2005 study of students in North America found that 7 percent of undergraduates admitted to turning in papers written by someone else, while 3 percent admitted to obtaining essays from online platforms. Cath Ellis, a researcher on the topic, said millions of essays are ordered online every year worldwide.

"It's a huge problem," said Tricia Bertram Gallant, director of the academic integrity office at the University of California, San Diego. "If we don't do anything about it, we will turn every accredited university into a diploma mill."

When such websites first emerged over a decade ago, they featured veiled references to tutoring and editing services, said Dr. Bertram Gallant, who also is a board member of the International Center for Academic Integrity. Now the sites are blatant.

"You can relax knowing that our reliable, expert writers will produce you a top quality and 100% plagiarism free essay that is written just for you, while you take care of the more interesting aspects of student life," reads the pitch from Academized, which charges about $15 a page for a college freshman's essay due in two weeks and $42 a page for an essay due in three hours.

"No matter what kind of academic paper you need, it is simple and secure to hire an essay writer for a price you can afford," promises EssayShark.com. "Save more time for yourself."

In an email, EssayShark said the company did not consider its services to be cheating, and that it warned students the essays are for "research and reference purposes only" and are not to be passed off as a student's own work. Representatives for Academized and Ace-MyHomework did not return emails and phone calls seeking comment.

A major scandal involving contract cheating in Australia caused university officials there to try to crack down on the practice. A similar effort to confront the industry has emerged in Britain, but not in the United States. Experts said that no federal law in the United States, or in Kenya, forbids the purchase or sale of academic papers.

Bill Loller, vice president of product management for Turnitin, a company that develops software to detect plagiarism, said some colleges have students who have never shown up for class or completed a single assignment. "They've contracted it all out," he said.

Contract cheating is harder to detect than plagiarism because ghostwritten essays will not be flagged when compared with a database of previously submitted essays; they are generally original works — simply written by the wrong person. But this year, Turnitin rolled out a new product called Authorship Investigate, which uses a host of clues — including sentence patterns and a document's metadata — to attempt to determine if a paper was written by the student who turned it in.

Some of the websites operate like eBay, with buyers and sellers bidding on specific assignments. Others operate like Uber, pairing desperate students with available writers. Either way, the identities and locations of both the writers and the students are masked from view, as are the colleges the assignments are for.

In Kenya, a country with a per capita annual income of about $1,700, successful writers can earn as much as $2,000 a month, according to Roynorris Ndiritu, 28, who said he has thrived writing essays. He graduated with a degree in civil engineering. But after years of applying unsuccessfully for jobs, he began writing for others full time. He has earned enough to buy a car and a piece of land.

In interviews with people in Kenya who said they had worked in contract cheating, many said they did not view the practice as unethical.

In a strange twist on globalization and outsourcing, some sites have begun to advertise their American ties, as more foreign writers have joined the industry. One site lists "bringing jobs back to America" as a key goal. American writers, who sometimes charge as much as $30 per page, say that they offer higher-quality service, without British spellings or idioms that might raise suspicion about an essay's authorship.

Ms. Mbugua, 25, the Kenyan university student, worked for as little as $4 a page. She said she began carrying a notebook, jotting

7　**contract ~ out**
「～を外注する」

13　**roll out** 「公表する」

17　**eBay** アメリカ最大のインターネットオークションサイト.

18　**Uber** アプリを利用したアメリカの配車サービス.

19　**available** 「求めに応じられる」

25　**civil engineering** 「土木工学」

35　**key goal** 「主要目標」

down vocabulary words she encountered in movies and novels to make her essays more valuable.

She lost her mother to diabetes in 2001, when she was in the second grade. She vowed to excel in school so that she would one day be able to support her younger brother and sister. 5

There were low points. During summer break, work slowed to a trickle. Once, she agonized so much over an American history paper about how the Great Depression ended that she rejected the job at the last minute, and had to pay an $18 fine.

Now Ms. Mbugua finds herself at a crossroads, unsure of what to 10 do next. She graduated from her university in 2018 and has sent her résumé to dozens of employers. Lately she has been selling kitchen utensils.

Ms. Mbugua said she never felt right about the writing she did in the names of American students and others. "I've always had 15 somehow a guilty conscience," she said.

"People say the education system in the U.S., U.K. and other countries is on a top notch," she said. "I wouldn't say those students are better than us," she said, later adding, "We have studied. We have done the assignments." 20

6 **low point** 「どん底 の時期」
8 **the Great Depression** 「世 界大恐慌」
9 **at the last minute** 「土壇場で」

Notes

1 2019 年 3 月，アメリカの名門大学の入学をめぐって大規模な不正があったことが発覚した．富裕層が自分の子供のために試験監督やスポーツチームのコーチに賄賂を支払い，入試を別室で有利に受けさせたり，スポーツ経験がないにもかかわらず経歴を詐称してスポーツ推薦枠で入学させたりした．この件で訴追された保護者は 40 人以上で，有名女優や弁護士 , 会社経営者らが名を連ねた．

2 オーストラリアで 2014 ～ 2015 年，16 の大学で 1000 人以上の学生が MyMaster というオンラインのレポート代行業者を利用して単位を取得していたことが判明した．何度も利用して複数の授業単位を取った学生や，ひとつのレポートに 1000 ドル支払った学生もいた．学生達にはその後，除籍や停学，単位や学位の取り消しなどの処罰が課された．

A: Word Match

Match the compounds to their description

1. Bribery Scheme		a. Lawyers acting on behalf of a country to bring cases against criminal actions.
2. Reception desk		b. The front table at which customers are welcomed into a building.
3. Financial trouble		c. Honest and ethical fulfillment of requirements in formal education.
4. Lucrative Profession		d. Actions done at a very large, mechanized level.
5. Federal prosecutors		e. An officially recognized institution of post-secondary education.
6. Industrial scale		f. A systematic plan to exchange illegal favors.
7. Money-back guarantees		g. Awareness of one's responsibility for a bad action.
8. Diploma mill		h. Written promises to give back invested cash if a product of service does not satisfy.
9. Academic integrity		i. A job that makes a lot of money.
10. Accredited university		j. Hiring out work that legally or morally should be done by oneself.
11. Contract cheating		k. An education factory. A school that freely gives lots of degrees with inadequate education and assessment.
12. Guilty conscience		l. Problems with money.

B: Comprehension Questions

1. What lucrative industry did Mary Mbugua join when she could not succeed in selling insurance policies and working at a reception desk?
2. Why are college admissions of wealthy Americans being scrutinized?
3. What is different about cheating in college now?
4. How have internet essay writing businesses become more sophisticated?
5. Where have such businesses expanded significantly?
6. How much money was Ms. Mbugua able to make in one month?
7. What percentage of North American undergraduates admit to turning in papers written by someone else?
8. Why is this a huge problem for academic integrity?
9. How much does the company Academized charge for papers?
10. Why can't universities stop ghostwritten essays?
11. How much is the per capita annual income of an average Kenyan compared to the monthly income of a successful writer?
12. How do most writers in Kenya feel about contract cheating compared to Ms. Mbugua?

C: Discussion Questions

1. Why is it dangerous for universities and society if many students cheat?
2. How would you feel if you knew your doctor or airline pilot cheated on his or her test?
3. Why would both Kenyans and Indians be good at writing English essays?
4. What do you think of the fact that people from developing countries such as Kenya are doing the homework of people in developed countries like the United States?
5. The historian Will Durant once wrote: "All history is big boots going upstairs, silk slippers going downstairs." What do you think this means?
6. An old adage says: "Steal from one essay it is called cheating, steal from many it is called scholarship." What do you think this means?

D: Research Questions

1. Look up the rates of plagiarism as U.S. universities.
2. Look up the rates of plagiarism in your country.
3. What famous American actresses were caught in the American college admissions bribery scheme in 2018?
4. Have there been any academic scandals in Japan? Find one and describe.
5. Imagine that everyone cheated on their tests, from engineers to truck drivers, from nurses to politicians. List some problems that might occur in society. (e.g collapsed bridges.)
6. List other jobs that people from developing countries do in or for developed countries?
7. What kind of jobs does Japan need immigrants for?
8. Number the following according to how hard you think each generation worked in the last 100 years. E. g. Your great grandparents, grandparents, parents and you. 1 for the hardest working. 4 for the laziest.

Unit **6**

In China, Daydreaming Students Are Caught on Camera

By Javier C. Hernández   April 25, 2017

A: Crossword

Match the words in the Word Bank to their descriptions to fill in the crossword.

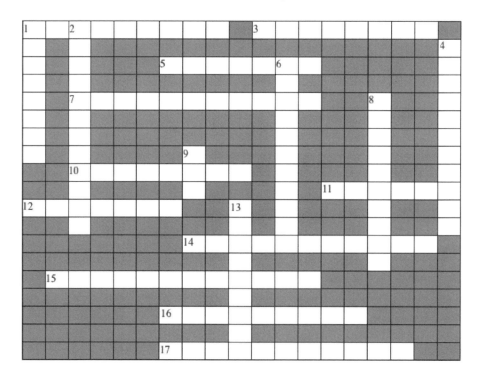

Word Bank

Censorship	Crowdsource	Daydreaming	Installed	Intrusion	Invading	Lax
Misbehaving	Monitor	Motivate	Privacy	Psychopaths	Security	Supervision
Surveillance	Threat	Transforming	Violation			

Across

1. (n.) Unwanted involvement. The act when someone enters a place or situation they are not wanted or expected.
3. (n.) The quality of being safe, free from danger, fear or anxiety.
5. (n.) The state of being secluded from the view of others. Freedom from unauthorized intrusion.
7. (n.) Overseeing the performance of a person or a group.
10. (v.) Inspire, prompt, give energy to do something.
11. (n.) A danger to. An expression of intention to inflict harm.
12. (v.) Surveillance. To keep an eye on, watch, supervise.
14. (adj.) Acting badly.
15. (n.) Keeping a close eye on someone.
16. (n.) The act of harming or failing to show proper respect for a person.
17. (adj.) Drifting off into wishful thoughts. Not paying attention.

Down

1. (v.) Present Participle. Entering forcefully into another's territory, intruding upon.
2. (v.) Present Participle. Changing.
4. (n.) Mentally unstable people with a lack of concern for others and criminal tendencies.
6. (v.) To call on many people to help fulfill a task.
8. (n.) The act of blocking materials deemed immoral or politically sensitive from the general public.
9. (adj.) Negligent, lazy, careless, slack.
13. (v.) Simple Past. Put in place. Set in order.

B: Discussion Questions

1. Do you like reality shows like Terrace House or Big Brother or Love Island?
2. Would you like to be on such a show?
3. What do you think about having cameras live-streaming in every classroom?
4. Would you like it? How would you feel?
5. Would it make you study harder?
6. Do you like to daydream? Or do you check your phone in class?
7. Would having cameras prevent you from doing so?

C: Research Activities

1. Write in the names of the 5 largest cities in China in the blanks.

2. Add the population inside the brackets below the name.

3. Draw in 2 rivers, the highest mountain range and the largest desert in China.

THE FIVE LARGEST CITIES IN CHINA

BEIJING — In the halls of Yuzhou No. 1 High School in central China, students refer to them simply as "the cameras." When the first bell sounds before 7 a.m., their fish-eye lenses spring to life, broadcasting live as students sit at their desks and measure geometric angles, pass notes or doze during breaks.

Before long, thousands of people — not just parents and teachers — are watching online, offering armchair commentary. "What is this boy doing? He's been looking around doing nothing, like a cat on a hot roof," one user wrote. "This one is playing with his phone!" added another, posting a screenshot.

As internet speeds have improved, live-streaming has become a cultural phenomenon in China, transforming online entertainment and everyday rituals like dating and dining. Now the nation's obsession with live video is invading its schools, and not everyone is happy about it.

Thousands of schools — public and private, from kindergarten to college — are installing webcams in classrooms and streaming live on websites that are open to the public, betting that round-the-clock supervision, even from strangers, will help motivate students.

School officials see the cameras as a way to improve student confidence and crowdsource the task of catching misbehaving pupils. Parents use the feeds to monitor their children's academic progress and spy on their friendships and romances. But many students see live-streaming as an intrusion, prompting a broader debate in China about privacy, educational ethics and the perils of helicopter parenting.

"I hate it," said Ding Yue, a 17-year-old senior at Yuzhou No. 1 High, in Xuchang, a city in Henan Province. "I feel like we are zoo animals."

Some experts warn that live-streaming in schools will make Chinese youth, already accustomed to the nation's extensive internet censorship and use of outdoor security cameras, even more sensitive to surveillance.

"If classrooms are under surveillance at all times, instruction will definitely be influenced by outside factors and the opinions of whoever is watching," said Xiong Bingqi, vice president of the 21st Century Education Research Institute, an influential Chinese think tank, who called the practice a violation of students' rights and a threat to academic freedom.

After a critical article on the subject recently in The Beijing

News, a prominent newspaper, several schools announced they were ending the broadcasts. But thousands of others chose to remain online and continue to draw a daily audience of cyber class monitors eager to report daydreaming students and lax teachers.

There are dozens of live-streaming platforms in China, and classroom feeds can be found on many of them. Anyone with an internet connection can visit and choose from thousands of live school feeds.

"When you tell them, 'It's possible your parents might be behind your back watching,' it's like a sword hanging over their heads," said Zhao Weifeng, the director of a private school in the eastern province of Jiangsu that installed cameras in its classrooms last year. "Having surveillance makes children behave better."

The Deep Blue Children Robot Center, a network of technology enrichment programs based in Beijing, said it had made live-streaming a central part of its teaching model. "A noble person shouldn't have anything to hide," said Jiang Jifa, a computer scientist and co-founder of the network.

In China's cutthroat education system, live-streaming has also found evangelists among G.P.A.-obsessed parents looking for new ways to push their children and schools eager to improve academic performance. "It helps students spend their time more efficiently and get into their dream universities," a parent of a senior at Yuzhou No. 1 High wrote recently in an online forum.

Webcams have proved especially popular at rural boarding schools, where live-streaming can be a vital link between children and parents, often migrants working in cities hundreds of miles away.

China is not the first to use internet-enabled cameras in classrooms. Private schools and charter schools in the United States have in recent years experimented with closed-circuit, private broadcasts to deter crime and misbehavior. Britain is testing body cameras for teachers in part to gather evidence for student disciplinary hearings.

But critics say Chinese schools have adopted live-streaming technology on an unheard-of scale and with few of the privacy protections.

Deng Xu, whose daughter attends an elite preschool in Beijing, said she understood the desire to keep an eye on children and their teachers at school, especially when they are very young. But she

3 cyber class monitor 「授業のサイバー監視装置」
5 live-streaming platform 「ライブストリーミングサービス」
12 province of Jiangsu 「江蘇（こうそ）省」
19 cutthroat 「激烈な」
20 evangelist 「熱烈な支持者」
G. P. A. -obsessed 「G. P. A. に取り憑かれた」
31 closed-circuit 「閉鎖回路の」特定の施設内だけの信号伝送システムのこと.
34 disciplinary hearing 「懲罰審理」

said at some point parents had to let go. "It's just sad to be watched all the time," she said. "Parents need to learn to be hands-off."

Han Xiao, a lawyer in Beijing, said that many schools were operating the cameras without the consent of parents and students and that public broadcasts posed a threat to student safety.

"Classrooms are enclosed spaces, so the activities of students like reading and eating snacks should be regarded as private," he said. "Living under surveillance and fear will hurt students' potential to grow."

10 **cutting edge** 「流行の最先端」

Live-streaming in general is on the cutting edge of entertainment in China, making stars of ordinary people as they use their phones to broadcast meals, candid monologues on the meaning of life and tutorials on subjects like applying makeup and rebuilding cars. The industry more than doubled in size in 2016 and is expected to generate $5 billion in revenue this year, largely through the sale of

16 **virtual gift** 「バーチャルギフト」→ Note 2

virtual gifts, according to Credit Suisse.

At Yuzhou No. 1 High, students now joke that their school should instead be called "Yuzhou No. 1 Prison." To avoid the camera's stare, they sometimes congregate in a blind spot near the front of the classroom, they said. "Who knows if there are any psychopaths watching?" asked Li Li, a junior.

The school did not respond to a request for comment.

Ding Yue, the senior, said live-streaming had also contributed to bullying at the school, recalling how a student was teased after classmates read that an online commenter had made fun of his looks. "Most students want to speak and fend for themselves, but we don't have the power," he said, when asked if students had complained to the school. "It's the business of grown-ups. We aren't allowed to talk about it."

Notes

1　ヘリコプターペアレントというのは子離れできない過干渉で過保護な親のこと．ヘリコプターで上空から常に子供を監視しながらボバリングし，何か異変があると急降下して子供を助けに行くイメージから名付けられた．

2　ライブストリーミング番組の中には，視聴者が配信者に対してバーチャルギフト（仮想の贈り物）を贈るという仕掛けを持つものがある．視聴者は予め仮想のコインを購入するなどし，画面上のアイコンをクリックしてリアルタイムでお気に入りの配信者に「投げ銭」のようにギフトを贈ることができる．贈られたギフトの一部は配信者の収入となる．配信の中身は楽器や歌，料理やゲームの腕前の披露などだが，雑談だけのものも多く，視聴者と配信者がサイト上で一緒に歌ったり日常的な会話を楽しんだりという双方向のコミュニケーションが売りになっている．

Post-reading

A: Word Match

Match the compounds to their description

1. Broadcasting live		a. A school that receives government funding, but is independent of the school system.
2. Armchair commentary		b. Continual, never ending observation, or watching-over of a group or individual.
3. Live-streaming		c. Transmitting real time events over television, radio or internet.
4. Cultural phenomenon		d. The opinions of people who are not directly involved, usually lacking expertise or experience.
5. Round-the-clock supervision		e. Frank, honest, open hearted talking by one person.
6. Educational ethics		f. Over cautious raising of children, always hovering over them to protect them.
7. Helicopter parenting.		g. Actions or systems set up to safeguard a person's right to personal space.
8. Charter schools		h. Continual transmission of events as they happen.
9. Unheard-of-scale		i. A trial or meeting concerning the disobedience of a worker or student.
10. Privacy protections		j. A surprising act or trend within a specific group of people.
11. Disciplinary hearings.		k. An unbelievable, never reached level.
12. Candid monologues		l. Morals related to school and learning.

B: Comprehension Questions

1. What has become a cultural phenomenon in China?
2. Where are web cameras for live streaming being installed?
3. Why are the Chinese betting that broadcasting students studying is a good thing?
4. How do students see and feel about this practice?
5. What did Xiong Bingqi, vice president of 21century Education Research Institute, call this practice?

6. Why do the heads of some schools like Zhao Weifeng and Jiang Jifa support the practice?
7. What other countries have used internet enabled cameras?
8. What do critics say is different in China?
9. How much money is the live-streaming Industry expected to generate this year?
10. What do students joke at Yuzhou No. 1 High School and what did Li Li, a junior, ask?

C: Discussion Questions

1. What do you think of China's having cameras live-streaming in every classroom?
2. Do you think having cameras in the classroom is a violation of your privacy rights?
3. Now there are more and more surveillance cameras around the streets, in shops etc. Many have facial recognition technology. Do you think this is a good thing? Debate the pros and cons.
4. Have you heard the term Helicopter parents? What other kinds of parenting are there?
5. Do your parents try to watch over everything you do?
6. When you have children, will you get them a phone, and will you use tracer apps to track their movements? Would you want to be able to see your children while they are at school?

D: Research Questions

1. Name 5 live-streaming shows (T.V. or internet) in Japan?
2. What is the live streaming Industry worth in Japan?
3. Look up the number of people making their living from youtubing. Who are the top 5?
4. What is the number of security cameras in the world?
5. What are the top 10 countries in terms of surveillance cameras?
6. How many cameras does Japan have approximately?
7. List some other kinds of security applications now being used.

IV

Different Destinations and Reasons for Travel

Unit 7

'Last Chance Travel' As the World Changes

By Julie Weed   March 5, 2018

Pre-reading

A: Crossword

Match the words in the Word Bank to their descriptions to fill in the crossword.

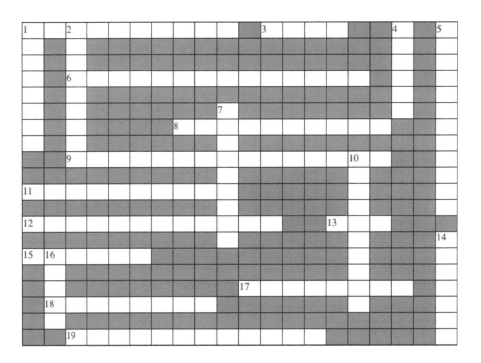

Word Bank

Adapt	Biodiversity	Conscious	Conservation	Cusp	Decline	Disappearing
Ecosystems	Excursions	Explorer	Glaciers	Hasten	Mitigation	Pristine
Raw	Statistic	Superintendents		Sustainability		Threatened
Vanish						

Across

1. (n.) Going out. Expeditions. Brief pleasure or reduced rate trips.
3. (n.) A turning point. Edge, or verge.
6. (n.) A resource that is capable of being used, or action able to be done, over and again without causing depletion.
8. (n.) The act of making something less severe, dangerous or damaging.
9. (n.) People who are in charge and have the official oversight to take care of something.
11. (n.) Complex communities of organisms in specific environments.
12. (n.) The amount of different species of plants and animals in an environment.
13. (adj.) In this case, undeveloped, natural state.
15. (v.) To disappear, pass from sight or existence.
17. (n.) Large bodies of ice spreading or receding on a land surface or valley.
18. (adj.) Fresh, clean, undamaged. Not spoiled or polluted. Similar to the original state.
19. (v.) Present participle. To go out of view or existence.

Down

1. (n.) A person who travels in search of scientific or geographic information.
2. (adj.) Awareness. Being mindfully awake. Perceiving or apprehending with a degree of controlled thought.
4. (v.) To speed up.
5. (n.) The careful preservation of something.
7. (n.) A number computed from sample populations, objects or situations.
10. (adj.) Facing danger of damage or extinction.
14. (n.) A state of being destroyed, or wasting away.
16. (v.) To modify to fit an environment or situation.

B: Discussion Questions

1. Where would you like to travel?
2. What's the most exotic place you have ever been to?
3. Do you think it is cool to have been somewhere your friends have not?
4. Have you ever seen an endangered species, like a black rhino, in real life?
5. What are some animals or places you think may no longer exist in your lifetime?
6. Do you think you should try to see these places or animals before they disappear?

C: Research Activities

1. Using clues from the names on the map or by researching, write in the names of the countries in the blank spaces marked 1.

2. Write the names of the province and state in the blanks spaces marked 2.

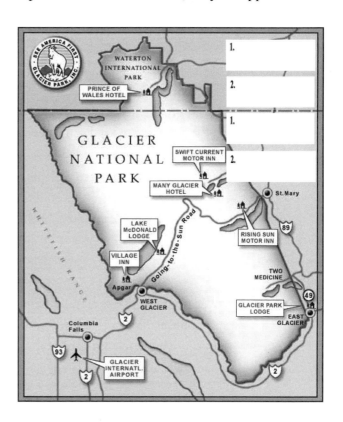

MAP 1. Glacier National Park

3. Write the names of the countries on the map in the blank spaces marked 3.
4. Write the names of the state and province/territory in the blank spaces marked 4.
5. Write the names of the bodies of water in the blank spaces marked 5.

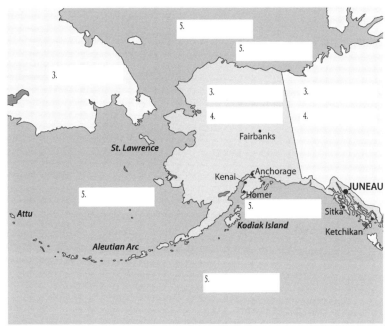

MAP 2. Kenai Fjords

1 **bucket list** 「生き
ているうちにやりたい
ことの一覧」

I t's a new kind of bucket list item known informally as "last chance travel."

Cuban street life fits into the category. So do African black rhinos and glaciers around the world. As local cultures and natural habitats are transformed by globalization, technology and climate change, a growing number of travelers want to experience them before they are irrevocably altered or vanish.

Amit Sankhala, the owner of Encounters Asia in New Delhi, has been guiding travelers, mostly from America, for the last 14 years. Now, he said, more of his clients are expressing the desire to see a place or a certain animal species before it's too late. They're "more and more conscious that things are disappearing."

Dan Austin, owner of the travel company Austin Adventures, said he fielded questions almost daily on the current state of glaciers in Alaska, the Canadian Rockies or Glacier National Park. The number of glaciers at Glacier National Park is down to 26, from about 150 in 1910, when the park was created.

That's the kind of statistic that keeps Ken Lyons of Ridgewood, N.J., traveling to ecosystems on three continents. At Exit Glacier in

15 **Canadian Rockies**
「カナディアン・ロッ
キー」
**Glacier National
Park** 「グレー
シャー国立公園」
19 **Exit Glacier in
Kenai Fjords
National Park**
「キナイ・フィヨルド
国立公園内のイグ
ジット氷河」

—58—

Kenai Fjords National Park: a sign marks the glacier's retreat.

jtstewartphoto by Getty Images

1 **physical marker**
   「標識」→ Note 1
2 **sign = physical marker**

5 **Death Valley**
   「デス・バレー」

10 **secretary of the interior** 「内務長官」→ Note 2
12 **address** 「取り組む」

16 **carbon footprint**
   「CO₂ 排出量」

18 **photographic safari** 「撮影旅行隊」

23 **Great Barrier Reef**
   「グレート・バリア・リーフ」

Kenai Fjords National Park in Alaska, physical markers show the glacier's retreat each year, and "as you walk up the trail the signs just get farther apart because a larger amount is melting each year," Mr. Lyons said.

This year, Mr. Lyons traveled to Death Valley in California to see the biodiversity there and the night sky, which is famous for stargazing. "You never know how things are going to change," he said.

Traveling to places that are threatened can help people understand what is at risk, said Sally Jewell, who was secretary of the interior under President Barack Obama. During her tenure, National Parks superintendents were asked to create plans to address the impact of climate change on their parks. The plans included ways to adapt, like building berms to reduce flooding risk that had increased because of climate change, and mitigation, like reducing the parks' carbon footprint by installing solar energy. The superintendents were also asked to tell visitors about changes at their parks.

Andy Biggs, who has led photographic safaris in Africa and other remote places for 15 years, said that while some of his clients are looking for a photographic trophy, others want the chance to experience the destination the way it is now. They want to see pristine places and threatened species, he said.

A survey of visitors to the Great Barrier Reef, off the coast of

Australia, found that nearly 70 percent said their desire "to see the reef before it's gone" was the primary reason for their journey.

Marilyn and Paul Schlansky of Cape Cod, Mass., said they liked to travel off the beaten path to destinations like Myanmar and Mongolia, where the cultures are changing. "It's hard to predict when something will disappear," Mr. Schlansky said. "You're not sure how much is changing until you show up."

On trips with the travel company Overseas Adventure Travel, the Schlanskys have gone on "Day in the Life" excursions that included making yogurt tea in a yurt, collecting dung for fuel and weaving. Local tour guides also take time to point out how modernity is creeping in, seeing how, for example, plastic water bottles have been collected and used as building materials.

Travelers want to do more than witness the habitats and ways of life that are changing, Mr. Sankhala said, so they seek out immersive experiences like eating in someone's home rather than in local restaurants. "They don't want to just look at a monument," he said. "They want to meet people attached to the history of that monument."

Melissa Bradley, who runs the boutique travel agency Indagare in New York, said she has taken small groups to destinations including Namibia, Rwanda, Bhutan and Madagascar. "It's magical to feel like an explorer, and that's a harder experience to come by now."

When a new destination opens or gains popularity, some travelers want to visit, before others discover it and change the destination's flavor, she said.

Ms. Bradley said she took a group to Iran. "People would come up to us on the street to ask about our lives and talk about their own," she said. Going to a place where authentic exchanges between cultures are still happening is a prize for travelers, she said.

Crowds can descend quickly. The number of foreign visitors to Iceland grew to about 1.8 million from about a million between 2014 and 2016, according to the Icelandic Tourist Board. About 4.7 million tourists visited Cuba in 2017, a significant increase over the previous year, despite hurricane damage in September. Mr. Austin said his clients want to get to Cuba "while it's still kind of raw." Ms. Bradley said that "some people feel like they already missed it."

While heaps of tourists can hasten a natural area's decline, Mr.

4 **off the beaten path** 「人里離れた」

16 **immersive** 「実体験できる」

20 **boutique** 「小規模な」

23 **come by** 「手に入れる」

5

10

15

20

25

30

35

40

Sankhala said tourism can be an important source of revenue in isolated areas. Tourists interested in remote destinations are typically also the kind who want to visit in a way that still promotes "conservation, sustainability and a low carbon footprint," he said.

Countries can also control the number of visitors and their impact. Costa Rica's ecotourism industry is a great example of this, Mr. Austin said. "They use their popularity to bring in funds while still preserving habitats and ecosystems."

"We have seen a huge increase in the number of people traveling to places on the cusp of great change," Ms. Bradley said.

Notes

1 イグジット氷河はキナイ・フィヨルド国立公園の中で人気の高い場所で，徒歩で氷河の手前まで近づくことができる．道中に 1926，1961，2010 などと年号を記した標識が立っていて，かつてその年には氷河の先端がそこにあったことを示している．地球温暖化で年を追うごとに氷河が急速に後退していることがわかる．

2 アメリカ合衆国内務省は，連邦政府所有の公有地と天然資源の管理責任を担う行政機関．野生生物の保護，国立公園の管理，河川や海岸，史跡の景観保全など，国内の自然遺産と文化遺産の保護を業務としている．

Post-reading

A: Word Match

Match the compounds to their description

1. Bucket-list		a. Changed beyond repair.
2. Natural habitats		b. Places not normally traveled to by many people.
3. Irrevocably altered		c. Vanishing places or things of wonder.
4. Current state		d. Original living places of animals and plants.
5. Carbon footprint		e. Totally absorbing events. Truly involved in another language or culture.
6. Off the beaten path		f. A government minister in charge of federal land and natural resources within the country.
7. Immersive experiences		g. Distant, hard to reach places to travel to.
8. Authentic exchanges		h. How things are now.
9. Disappearing marvels		i. Noticeable or considerable rise.
10. Secretary of the interior		j. The amount of CO_2 created by a person's, country's or species' way of life.
11. Significant increase		k. True and honest sharing (of words or cultures)
12. Remote destinations.		l. Things you desire to see or do before you die.

B: Comprehension Questions

1. What kinds of things constitute "last chance travel"?
2. Why do people want to see such things?
3. What does Amit Sankhala say people are more and more conscious of?
4. How many glaciers are there now at Glacier National Park compared to in 1910?
5. How does traveling to such threatened places help, according to Sally Jewell, Obama's secretary of the interior?
6. What kinds of plans did superintendents create in order to adapt to and mitigate climate change in the National Parks?
7. How has modernity been creeping into places off the beaten path like Mongolia and Myanmar?
8. What kinds of "immersive experiences" are people looking for?
9. What feeling is magical but harder to experience now?
10. How many foreigners visited Iceland in 2016 compared to 2014?
11. What is a problem with heaps of tourists visiting an area, according to Mr. Sankhala?
12. However, what does Dan Austin say are the positive sides of ecotourism?

C: Discussion Questions

1. What is on your bucket list?
2. What is something you would like to see before it vanishes?
3. Have you ever felt like an explorer? Describe the experience.
4. Do you think it is good for people to go to visit endangered animals and places? What are the problems with such travel?
5. Do you watch any travel shows? Which ones? What do you like about them?
6. Plane flight is one of the largest contributors to CO_2 emissions. In Sweden most people have decided to stop flying in order to reduce their carbon footprint. Is this a good idea?
7. How big do you think your carbon footprint is and what can you do to reduce it?

D: Research Questions

1. Make a list of some endangered species.
2. Make a list of natural places that are threatened by modernity and pollution.
3. How much CO_2 does one plane taking off emit?
4. Which countries in the world are the top 10 emitters of CO_2?
5. How does Japan rate in terms of CO_2 emissions?
6. List some ways in which we may reduce our CO_2 emissions.

Unit 8

Chinese Babies, Born Into Canadian Citizenship

By Dan Bilefsky   Dec. 31, 2018

Pre-reading

A: Crossword

Match the words in the Word Bank to their descriptions to fill in the crossword.

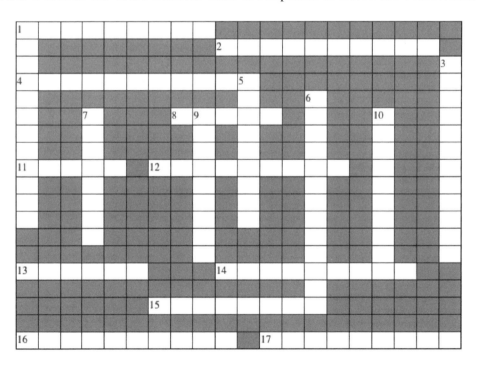

Word Bank

Abolished	Absconded	Authoritarian	Citizenship	Debasing	Haven	Influx
Lactation	Legal	Maternity	Mobilizing	Obstetrician	Petition	
Pregnancy	Recuperate	Unethical	Unscrupulous	Vigilantes		

Across

1. (adj.) Not acting according to acceptable social or professional standards.
2. (n.) People who take the law into their own hands and attack people they believe are guilty of breaking the law.
4. (n.) The status including the rights and duties of a member of a state or political group.
8. (n.) A safe place or shelter.
11. (adj.) Permitted by law, accepted rules.
12. (n.) The secretion of milk from the breasts for feeding infants following birth.
13. (n.) The process of flowing into something, like refugees into a country.
14. (v.) Past Participle. To get rid of, stop, do away with.
15. (n.) A formal message or request submitted to an authority, often including a collection of signatures.
16. (v.) Present Participle. Making ready for action, use or war. To cause to move around.
17. (n.) The state and period of being pregnant; the quality, act and relationship of motherhood.

Down

1. (adj.) Without principles or morals.
3. (n.) A doctor specializing in childbirth and pre and post-natal care of the mother.
5. (n.) The gestation period of a baby; the period from conception to birth when a woman carries a developing fetus in her womb.
6. (adj.) Characteristic of absolute rule. The dictatorial demanding of unquestioning obedience.
7. (v.) Present Participle. To corrupt, dilute or lower the value of something by adding inferior ingredients, or of someone through immoral actions or advice.
9. (v.) Simple past. To run away, bolt, escape with.
10. (v.) To recover, regain or make up for. To get over an illness or shock.

B: Discussion Questions

1. If a baby is born in Japan, does it get Japanese citizenship, even if the parents are not Japanese?
2. If you could get citizenship to another country, in addition to your own, which country would you like to become a citizen of?
3. How about for your child? Would you like your child to have citizenship in another country?
4. How do you feel about more immigrants coming to Japan?
5. Do you mind if they use the Japanese health system while here?

C: Research Activities

1. What country is the map below from?

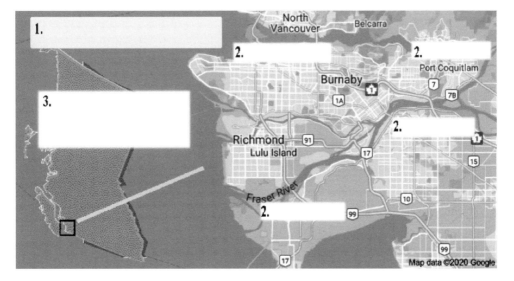

2. Fill in the blanks: What are the names of the cities?
3. Fill in the blank: What is the name of the province?

RICHMOND, British Columbia — Melody Bai arrived in Vancouver from China in the late stages of pregnancy with one goal: to give birth to a Canadian baby.

Awaiting her was an elaborate ecosystem catering to pregnant women from China, including a spacious "baby house" where she spent four months, attended to by a Mandarin-speaking housekeeper.

Caregivers offered free breast massages to promote lactation, outings to the mall, lectures on childbirth with other Chinese mothers-to-be and excursions for high tea.

"It's an investment in my child's education," Ms. Bai, a 28-year-old flight attendant, said by phone from Shanghai, after returning to China with her newborn and passport in hand. "We chose Canada because of its better natural and social environment."

Ms. Bai is part of a growing phenomenon in Canada known as birth tourism, which is generating political opposition and mobilizing self-appointed vigilantes determined to stop it.

It is perfectly legal.

Under the principle of jus soli — the right of the soil — being born in Canada confers automatic citizenship. But as more pregnant women arrive each month to give birth, some Canadians are protesting that they are gaming the system, testing the limits of tolerance and debasing the notion of citizenship.

In Richmond, a city outside Vancouver where about 53 percent of its roughly 200,000 residents are ethnic Chinese, nonresident mothers account for one in five births at the Richmond Hospital, the largest number of nonresident births of any hospital in the country.

"Birth tourism may be legal, but it is unethical and unscrupulous," said Joe Peschisolido, a Liberal member of Parliament in Richmond, who brought a petition against the practice to Ottawa, the capital.

The practice underlines how Canada, and British Columbia in particular, has become a favored haven for well-heeled Chinese seeking a refuge for wealth and kin away from authoritarian China.

At least 30 other countries, including the United States, Mexico and Brazil, grant automatic birthright citizenship. Others like

5

10

15

20

25

30

35

4　**ecosystem**　「（ビジネス上の）エコシステム」→ Note 1
catering to ~「～の要望に応える」
8　**lactation**「母乳の分泌」
10　**mother-to-be**「妊婦」

16　**birth tourism**「バースツーリズム，出産旅行」
17　**self-appointed vigilante**「自警団員と称する人」
19　**jus soli**「出生地主義」

22　**game**「悪用する」

25　**ethnic Chinese**「中国系市民」

29　**Liberal**「自由党」
30　**petition against ~**「～に反対する嘆願書」

34　**refuge**「逃げ場，安全地帯」
36　**birthright citizenship**「生得市民権」

Britain and Australia have tightened their laws by requiring that at least one parent be a citizen or permanent resident at the time of the child's birth.

The Conservative Party has endorsed a nonbinding motion calling for unconditional birthright citizenship to be abolished.

In the recent report, from the Institute for Research on Public Policy, Andrew Griffith, a former director general at the government department responsible for immigration, showed that the number of children born to nonresidents in Canada was at least five times as high as previously thought — close to 1,500 to 2,000 annually.

Mr. Griffith argues that Canada intended birthright citizenship for those who wanted to live in and contribute to the country. "Since those engaging in birth tourism have no or barely any real link to Canada," he said, "the practice is challenging a very Canadian value of fair play."

With its sprawling Chinese food markets, Chinese-language newspapers and large number of caregivers speaking Mandarin, Richmond has become ground zero for birth tourists from China.

About two dozen baby houses are in operation. Some operate openly while others work under licenses as tour agencies or present themselves as holiday rentals. Some are in homes. Others are in apartments. Many are booked through agents and brokers in China.

In a visit to one, the Baoma Inn, a modern house across from a park, a woman in the late stages of pregnancy could be seen in a second-floor window. A young man who answered the door confirmed that the inn was a baby house before another angrily slammed the door.

But during a telephone call in Mandarin inquiring about the Inn's services, a man said it offered a one-stop package including "guaranteed appointments" with "the No. 1 obstetrician in British Columbia," who spoke Mandarin and had "a zero accident rate."

Customers usually stay for three months, he said, including one month after the birth, to allow time to apply for a passport for the newborn and to recuperate, as is the Chinese custom.

He added that his agency had seven sales offices in China. The bill for a three-month stay at a two-bedroom apartment, not including meals and prenatal care, is about 25,000 Canadian dollars ($18,331).

"The women all go back to China," he said. "They don't enjoy any social benefits from the Canadian government and don't need

---

Margin glossary:

2 **permanent resident** 「永住権保持者」→ Note 2

4 **Conservative Party** 「保守党」 **endorse** 「採択する」 **nonbinding motion** 「拘束力のない決議案」

7 **director general** 「長官」

8 **responsible for ~** 「～を担当する」

18 **ground zero** 「中心地」

20 **present oneself as ~** 「～だとみせかける」

21 **holiday rental** 「貸別荘，貸家」

25 **answer the door** 「ドアを開けて応対する」

29 **one-stop package** 「1 か所ですべてが揃うツアー」

36 **bill** 「費用」

39 **enjoy** 「享受する」

In Richmond, which is outside Vancouver, about 71 percent of roughly 200,000 residents are of Asian descent.

Alana Paterson for The New York Times

写真：The New York Times/Redux/ アフロ

it."

Some Richmond residents say birth tourism is undermining the community's social fabric. Kerry Starchuk, who spearheaded the petition championed by Mr. Peschisolido, documents baby houses in her neighborhood and passes the information on to the local news media and city officials.

Ms. Starchuk complains that birth tourists bump local mothers from maternity wards, a concern echoed by some local nurses, and get access to public services without paying taxes. She also said the so-called "anchor babies" threatened to burden Canada by emigrating and studying here, and sponsoring their parents to become permanent residents.

The issue has become conflated with resentment in the Vancouver area against soaring housing prices, which some residents blame on an influx of wealthy Chinese.

But Ms. Bai, who had her baby in Vancouver in February, said that given the hefty price she had paid to give birth here — 60,000 Canadian dollars, including housing and hospitalization — she was subsidizing the Canadian health care system and contributing to the local economy. "My child won't be enjoying any Canadian health

3　**social fabric**　「社会構造」
4　**document**　「記録する」

8　**maternity ward**「産科病棟」

10　**anchor baby**　「アンカーベビー」→ Note 3

17　**given ～**　「～を考慮すると」

19　**health care system**「医療制度」

benefits, as we are living in China," she said.

Since her son is Canadian, however, she and her husband, a pilot, could save on tuition fees at an international school in Shanghai. Her son could also later attend a Canadian university at the discounted local rate. Eventually, the entire family could emigrate to Canada.

Some first- and second-generation immigrants oppose birth tourists for jumping the queue. Wendy Liu, a Richmond resident of 11 years, said, "I don't think it is fair to come here, give birth and leave."

Birth tourism at Richmond Hospital recently came under the spotlight because of a so-called "million dollar baby."

A nonresident, Yan Xia, gave birth there, racked up a bill of 312,595 Canadian dollars in maternity and neonatal care for her newborn because of complications, and then absconded without paying the bill, according to a civil claim the hospital filed at British Columbia's Supreme Court in April, six years after Ms. Xia gave birth.

Including six years' worth of interest, Ms. Xia's bill would amount to about 1.2 million Canadian dollars.

Notes

1 エコシステムとは，もとは自然界の生態系を表す言葉で，ある地域の生物が互いに依存しあいながら生態を維持していくさまを言う．経済やビジネス上で使われる場合は，ある業界内で製品やサービスを出し合って連携し，収益を維持して互いに利益を得るシステムのことをさす．

2 permanent resident というのは，国籍は外国だがその国に永住して働くことができる人のこと．選挙権はなくその国のパスポートも持っていない．一方，citizen はその国の国籍を持っている人のこと．

3 出生地主義を取っている国で子供を産むと，その子供は自動的に市民権が得られ，その家族にも在留許可がおりる．そういう目的で産んだ子供のことをアンカーベビーと呼ぶ．船を留めておくための錨（anchor）からきている．

4 上海にはアメリカ系，イギリス系，カナダ系など多くのインターナショナルスクールがある．英語を母語としない多国籍の子供が通う学校もあれば，ある国の在外教育機関として主にその国出身の子供を受け入れる学校もある．後者の場合，例えばカナダ系インターナショナルスクールであれば，在外教育機関という役割に基づき，カナダ国籍を持っていると授業料が安くなるメリットがある．

A: Word Match

Match the compounds to their description

1. Elaborate ecosystem		a. A party's or people's reaction to government policies.	
2. Growing phenomenon		b. A group's or country's conditions and attitudes.	
3. Political opposition		c. People allowed to stay in a country forever, but who do not have full citizenship.	
4. Gaming the system		d. A complex environment of support.	
5. Well-heeled		e. Infants born in a country different from their parents, used to acquire citizenship for the whole family.	
6. Social environment		f. The tending of newly born babies and their mothers.	
7. Anchor babies		g. The granting of full rights in a country based on being born there regardless of the origin and citizenship of one's parents.	
8. Permanent residents		h. An expanding remarkable development.	
9. Neonatal care		i. Assured reservations.	
10. Prenatal care		j. Taking advantage of a society's social benefits.	
11. Guaranteed appointments		k. The tending of infants and mothers before birth.	
12. Unconditional birthright citizenship		l. rich.	

B: Comprehension Questions

1. What was Melody Bai's one goal in going to Richmond B.C.?
2. What awaited her in Canada?
3. What do the caregivers at the "baby house" offer her?
4. Why did she choose Canada to give birth to her child?
5. What is the name of this growing phenomenon?
6. What does jus soli mean and what does it confer?
7. Why are some Canadians protesting this phenomenon?
8. What percentage of residents of Richmond, British Columbia, are ethnic Chinese?
9. Why does Kerry Starchuk complain against these "anchor babies?"
10. What other problem has this issue become conflated with?
11. What other countries grant automatic birthright citizenship?
12. How many children are born to nonresidents in Canada annually?

C: Discussion Questions

1. What do you think of automatic birthright citizenship?
2. What kinds of problems may arise from it?
3. Why do you think some countries offer it?
4. Do you think Japan needs more immigrants?
5. If you could choose, from where and what kind immigrants do you want?

D: Research Questions

1. Does Japan grant automatic birthright citizenship?
2. List 10 countries that give automatic birthright citizenship.
3. List 5 potential benefits and 5 problems of automatic birthright citizenship.
4. How many Korean nationals live in Japan now?
5. What are the rights and limitations for Koreans born in Japan?
6. List 5 other kinds of "tourism" that are different from just going to sightsee.

V

Technology: Transportation to or from Happiness?

Unit 9
Human Contact Is Now a Luxury Good

By Nellie Bowles   March 23, 2019

A: Crossword

Match the words in the Word Bank to their descriptions to fill in the crossword.

Word Bank

Animation	Anticipated	Artifice	Association	Avatar	Depression	Disturbingly
Emotes	Faith	Inadequate	Isolation	Luxury	Mediated	Nonprofit
Outpacing	Proliferating	Retired	Signal	Tablet	Tactile	

Across

1. (n.) A relationship.
5. (adj.) Perceptible by touch.
7. (n.) Belief and trust in God and/or the traditional doctrines of religion; belief in something for which there is no proof.
10. (n.) False, fake. A clever trick.
11. (n.) A feeling of sadness, dejection, and anxiety.
13. (v.) To express, display feelings.
14. (adj.) Not enough. Not good enough.
15. (n.) Something that provides pleasure but is not necessary.
16. (v.) Past Participle. Act as a go between people to ease relations.
17. (n.) The condition of being alone, segregated from others. Solitary.
18. (v). Present Participle. To outdo. Surpass in speed.
19. (n.) An electronic image representing a character, that is manipulated by a user.

Down

1. (adj.) Expected or looking forward to.
2. (adv.) Shockingly. Upsetting to the mind's sense of calmness.
3. (n.) A cartoon. A moving drawing.
4. (adj.) Stopped working. Usually at the end of one's career.
6. (n.) A flat, rectangular computer device.
8. (adj.) Not conducted for the purpose of making monetary gain.
9. (v.) Present participle. Growing rapidly increasing, multiplying.
12. (n.) A symbol. An object that conveys information.

B: Discussion Questions

1. Do you ever feel lonely?
2. If so, what do you do to face the loneliness?
3. Do you think the internet helps you deal with loneliness or makes you more lonely?
4. Do you like robots, like AIBO?
5. Do you think that a robot or computer screen avatar can fulfill our human needs and make us less lonely?
6. Are your grandparents lonely? Do you think old people living alone would like a robot or avatar to keep them company?

C: Research Activities

1. Look at the graph below. How do you feel after interacting on social media? Does it improve your relations with friends or weaken them?

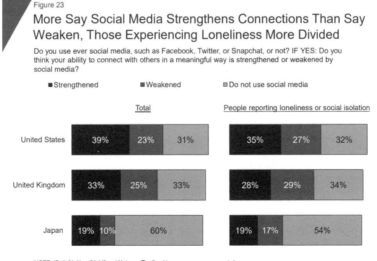

Figure 23

More Say Social Media Strengthens Connections Than Say Weaken, Those Experiencing Loneliness More Divided

Do you use ever social media, such as Facebook, Twitter, or Snapchat, or not? IF YES: Do you think your ability to connect with others in a meaningful way is strengthened or weakened by social media?

■ Strengthened   ■ Weakened   ▨ Do not use social media

	Total			People reporting loneliness or social isolation		
United States	39%	23%	31%	35%	27%	32%
United Kingdom	33%	25%	33%	28%	29%	34%
Japan	19%	10%	60%	19%	17%	54%

NOTE: "Both/Neither (Vol.)" and Not sure/Declined to answer responses not shown.
SOURCE: Kaiser Family Foundation/The Economist Survey on Loneliness and Social Isolation in the United States, the United Kingdom, and Japan (conducted April–June 2018)

2. Take a quick survey in your class. Ask ten students the same question and see how they feel. Write S for Strengthened and W for Weakened.

3. Write a sentence based on the information from your survey: E.g. 6 out of 10 students feel S (or W) social relations after using social media.

SAN FRANCISCO — Bill Langlois has a new best friend. She is a cat named Sox. She lives on a tablet, and she makes him so happy that when he talks about her arrival in his life, he begins to cry.

All day long, Sox and Mr. Langlois, who is 68 and lives in a low-income senior housing complex in Lowell, Mass., chat. Mr. Langlois worked in machine operations, but now he is retired. With his wife out of the house most of the time, he has grown lonely.

Sox talks to him about his favorite team, the Red Sox, after which she is named. She plays his favorite songs and shows him pictures from his wedding. And because she has a video feed of him in his recliner, she chastises him when she catches him drinking soda instead of water.

Mr. Langlois knows that Sox is artifice, that she comes from a start-up called Care.Coach. He knows she is operated by workers around the world who are watching, listening and typing out her responses, which sound slow and robotic. But her consistent voice in his life has returned him to his faith.

"I found something so reliable and someone so caring, and it's allowed me to go into my deep soul and remember how caring the

6   **housing complex** 「団地」
7   **machine operation** 「機械作業」

11   **video feed** 「ビデオ画像」

14   **artifice** 「巧妙な造りもの」

16   **type out** 「(画面に) 打ち込む」

Mr. Langlois's new friend, Sox the cat, lives on a tablet.

—76—

Lord was," Mr. Langlois said. "She's brought my life back to life."

Sox has been listening. "We make a great team," she says.

Sox is a simple animation; she barely moves or emotes, and her voice is as harsh as a dial tone. But little animated hearts come up around her sometimes, and Mr. Langlois loves when that happens.

Mr. Langlois is on a fixed income. To qualify for Element Care, a nonprofit health care program for older adults that brought him Sox, a patient's countable assets must not be greater than $2,000.

Such programs are proliferating. And not just for the elderly.

Life for anyone but the very rich — the physical experience of learning, living and dying — is increasingly mediated by screens.

Not only are screens themselves cheap to make, but they also make things cheaper. Any place that can fit a screen in (classrooms, hospitals, airports, restaurants) can cut costs. And any activity that can happen on a screen becomes cheaper. The texture of life, the tactile experience, is becoming smooth glass.

The rich do not live like this. The rich have grown afraid of screens. They want their children to play with blocks, and tech-free private schools are booming. Humans are more expensive, and rich people are willing and able to pay for them. Conspicuous human interaction — living without a phone for a day, quitting social networks and not answering email — has become a status symbol.

All of this has led to a curious new reality: Human contact is becoming a luxury good. As more screens appear in the lives of the poor, screens are disappearing from the lives of the rich. The richer you are, the more you spend to be offscreen.

Milton Pedraza, the chief executive of the Luxury Institute, advises companies on how the wealthiest want to live and spend, and what he has found is that the wealthy want to spend on anything human. "What we are seeing now is the luxurification of human engagement," Mr. Pedraza said.

Anticipated spending on experiences such as leisure travel and dining is outpacing spending on goods, according to his company's research, and he sees it as a direct response to the proliferation of screens. "Now education, health care stores, everyone, is starting to look at how to make experiences human," Mr. Pedraza said. "The human is very important right now."

This is a swift change. Since the 1980s personal computer boom, having technology at home and on your person had been a sign of wealth and power. Early adopters with disposable income rushed to get the newest gadgets and show them off. The first Apple Mac shipped in 1984 and cost about \$2,500 (in today's dollars, \$6,000). Now the very best Chromebook laptop costs \$470.

"Pagers were important to have because it was a signal that you were an important, busy person," said Joseph Nunes, chairman of the marketing department at the University of Southern California.

Today, he said, the opposite is true: "If you're truly at the top of the hierarchy, you don't have to answer to anyone. They have to answer to you."

The joy — at least at first — of the internet revolution was its democratic nature. Facebook is the same Facebook whether you are rich or poor. Gmail is the same Gmail. And it's all free. And as studies show that time on these advertisement-supported platforms is unhealthy, it all starts to seem déclassé, like drinking soda or smoking cigarettes, which wealthy people do less than poor people.

Screen exposure starts young. And children who spend more than two hours a day looking at a screen get lower scores on thinking and language tests, according to a study on brain development that the National Institutes of Health is supporting. Most disturbingly, the study is finding that the brains of children who spend a lot of time on screens are different. For some kids, there is premature thinning of their cerebral cortex. In adults, one study found an association between screen time and depression.

A toddler who learns to build with virtual blocks in an iPad game gains no ability to build with actual blocks, according to Dimitri Christakis, a pediatrician at Seattle Children's Hospital.

In small towns around Wichita, Kan., where school budgets have been so tight that the State Supreme Court ruled them inadequate, classes have been replaced by software, much of the academic day now spent in silence on a laptop. In Utah, thousands of children do a brief, state-provided preschool program at home via laptop.

Tech companies worked hard to get public schools to buy into programs that required schools to have one laptop per student, arguing that it would better prepare children for their screen-based future. But this idea isn't how the people who actually build the screen-based future raise their own children.

In Silicon Valley, time on screens is increasingly seen as unhealthy. Here, the popular elementary school is the local Waldorf School, which promises a back-to-nature, nearly screen-free education.

So as wealthy kids are growing up with less screen time, poor kids are growing up with more. Human engagement could become a new class marker.

Separating from screens is harder for the poor and middle class. Even if someone is determined to be offline, that is often not possible. 5

In airplanes coach seat backs have screen ads autoplaying. Public school parents might not want their kids learning on screens, but that is not an option when many classes are now built on one-to-one laptop programs. There is a small movement to pass a "right to disconnect" bill, which would allow workers to turn their phones 10 off, but for now a worker can be punished for going offline and not being available.

There is also the reality that in our culture of increasing isolation, in which so many of the traditional gathering places and social 15 structures have disappeared, screens are filling a crucial void.

Many enrolled in the avatar program at Element Care were failed by the humans around them or never had a community in the first place, and they became isolated, said Cely Rosario, the occupational therapist who frequently checks in on participants. 20 Poor communities have seen their social fabric fray the most, she said.

The technology behind Sox is quite simple: a tablet with an ultrawide-angle fisheye lens attached to the front. None of the people operating the avatars are in the United States; they mostly 25 work in the Philippines and Latin America.

The Care.Coach office is a warrenlike space above a massage parlor in Millbrae, Calif., on the edge of Silicon Valley. Victor Wang, the 31-year-old founder and chief executive, opens the door, and as he's walking in he tells me that they just stopped a suicide. 30 Patients often say they want to die, he said, and the avatar is trained to then ask if they have an actual plan of how to do it.

The voice is whatever the latest Android text-to-speech reader is. Mr. Wang said people can form a bond very easily with anything that talks with them. 35

Mr. Wang knows how attached patients become to the avatars. He does not try to limit the emotional connection between patient and avatar. "If they say, 'I love you,' we'll say it back," he said. "With some of our clients, we'll say it first if we know they like hearing it." 40

7 **coach** 「エコノミークラス」

11 **bill** 「法案」

16 **crucial void** 「大きな孤独感」

18 **fail** 「見捨てる」

20 **occupational therapist** 「作業療法士」

21 **fray** 「ほころびる」

24 **fisheye lens** 「魚眼レンズ」

33 **whatever ~** 「~のようなもの」
   text-to-speech reader 「テキスト読み上げ装置」

1   **pilot program**
「試験的プログラ
ム」

5   **health care
program** 「医療
サービスプログラム」

8   **motorized stand**
「電動式スタンド」
roll into 「ゴロゴ
ロと入ってくる」

9   **a doctor on a video
feed** .... → Note 3

Early results have been positive. In Lowell's first small pilot programs, patients with avatars needed fewer nursing visits, went to the emergency room less often and felt less lonely. One patient who had frequently gone to the emergency room for social support largely stopped when her avatar arrived, saving the health care program an estimated $90,000.

For a sense of where things could be headed, look to the town of Fremont, Calif. There, a tablet on a motorized stand recently rolled into a hospital room, and a doctor on a video feed told a patient, Ernest Quintana, 78, that he was dying.

Back in Lowell, Sox has fallen asleep, which means her eyes are closed and a command center somewhere around the world has tuned into other seniors and other conversations. Mr. Langlois's wife wants a digital pet, and his friends do too, but this Sox is his own. He strokes her head on the screen to wake her up.

Notes

1 アメリカには日本の介護保険制度のような高齢者に対する公的介護サービスはなく，PACE (program of all-inclusive care for the elderly) と呼ばれる NPO プログラムが州政府の承認を得て高齢者に介護支援を提供している．PACE の目的は心身に慢性疾患のある高齢者が住み慣れた地域で在宅のまま療養生活を続けることであり，訪問看護，デイケア通所，クリニック受診，栄養指導，リハビリ，リクリエーションなどのケアプランを作成し実行してくれる．文中の Element Care は PACE に認定されているプログラムのひとつ．

2 シリコンバレーはカリフォルニア州サンフランシスコ市南部のパロアルト，サンタクララ，サンノゼ周辺地域を呼ぶときの通称．アップル，インテル，ヒューレットパッカード，フェイスブック，グーグルなど半導体や情報通信の関連企業が数多く集まり，IT 産業の最先端技術を産み出している．

3 カリフォルニア州フレモントに住む Ernest Quintana さんは肺疾患で入院中だったが，容体が悪化したある日，病室に入ってきたロボットのビデオ画面を通して，治療のためにできることはもうないと医師から告げられたという．彼は翌日に亡くなった．その後孫娘がこの話をメディアに語り，尊厳を欠いた病院の対応のまずさを訴えた．

Post-reading

A: Word Match

Match the compounds to their description

1. Low-income		a. Elderly people's group home.
2. Senior housing		b. Access to or time spent using a computer, tablet or smart phone.
3. Tactile experience		c. A possession that shows off the owner's wealth.
4. Status symbol		d. The custom and social practice of accepting or causing the separation of people from others.

5. Luxury good		e. Money leftover after paying all one's bills that can be used for purchasing anything desired.
6. Disposable income		f. The grey surface area of the brain that coordinates sensory and motor information.
7. Cerebral cortex		g. A medical professional who helps people with physical impairments deal with daily life.
8. Screen exposure		h. Small salary, poorly paid.
9. Culture of isolation		i. A product that is valuable but not necessary.
10. Occupational therapist		j. The glass eye of a camera with a wide-angled view.
11. Social fabric		k. The process of observing and participating in reality through touch.
12. Fisheye lens		l. The invisible bonds that make up a community.

B: Comprehension Questions

1. Who is Sox?
2. Who is Bill Langlois?
3. Why does Bill like Sox?
4. Everybody's life is being increasingly mediated by screens, except for who?
5. Why are screens increasing in our lives?
6. What has become a status symbol?
7. What do the rich want to spend their money on?
8. How much did the first computers in 1984 cost in today's dollar, compared with a Chromebook laptop today?
9. What happens to the brains of children who spend a lot of time on screens?
10. What do the schools of Silicon Valley promise for the children whose parents who build computers?
11. What crucial void are screens filling?
12. How much money have avatars saved the health care program in the case of one patient?

C: Discussion Questions

1. Are you close to your grandparents? Do you see them often?
2. Will you take care of your parents when they are older?
3. Do you think it is good to leave old people or children alone with computers for long periods?
4. Can computer replace family and health care workers in this way?
5. What do you think of the problems of Hikikomori and Kodokushi?
6. How can we make society less lonely in the future?
7. Were you surprised that the rich and Silicon Valley professionals are against screen time for themselves and their children?
8. What are some other things that were once the privilege of the rich, like computers, but now everyone has?

D: Research Questions

1. What is the percentage of old people living in senior homes in Japan?
2. What is the percentage of computer use among the young compared to the elderly?
    The old :   The young:
3. What are the percentage of old and young in Japan who feel lonely?
    The old :   The young:
4. List the 5 loneliest and 5 least lonely countries in the world.
5. List the countries with the best education systems and if they use computers.
6. List the countries with the best social network for the elderly.

Unit **10**

With Cloning, Pet Owners in China Need Never Say Goodbye

By Sui-Lee Wee   Sept. 4, 2019

A: Crossword

Match the words in the Word Bank to their descriptions to fill in the crossword.

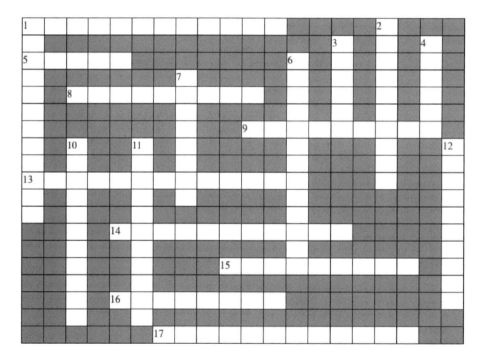

Word Bank

Accelerating	Anticipation	Bioethicist	Buried	Clone	Controversial
Emergence	Feline	Genetics	Harvested	Implanted	Irreplaceable
Know-how*	Laboratory	Miscarriages	Solidifying	Transplant	Unregulated

*Include hyphen when filling in crossword.

Across

1. (n.) The act of looking forward, especially to pleasurable expectation.
5. (n.) A genetic copy of an individual from one cell.
8. (n.) The act of coming out, newly formed or becoming prominent.
9. (v.) Past Participle. Gathered, hunted, removed or extracted from.
13. (adj.) Not able to have something else instead of the original and deliver same satisfaction.
14. (n.) A person concerned with the morality of biological research and applications.
15. (v.) Simple past. To insert into living tissue.
16. (n.) Expertise, skills, experience, intellectual and practical ability.
17. (n.) Sudden deaths and expulsion of fetuses before they reach successful development.

Down

1. (adj.) Speeding up.
2. (n.) A place equipped for scientific research, experiments, testing and analysis.
3. (adj.) Relating to or of cats and the cat family. Resembling a cat.
4. (v.) Simple Past. To dispose of by putting in the earth.
6. (adj.) Disputable, inspiring opposing views.
7. (n.) A branch of biology that deals with hereditary DNA and variations of organisms.
10. (adj.) Not controlled by laws or rules.
11. (v.) Present Participle. Becoming harder, more settled or certain.
12. (v.) To move something, or oneself, from one place and settle in another, such as an organ from one person to another.

B: Discussion Questions

1. Do you have a pet? What kind?
2. Which do you prefer cats or dogs?
3. If your pet died, or if you have had a pet that died, would you want to replace it with another different pet?
4. If you could clone the exact same pet, would you?
5. Do you think cloning is good or bad?
6. What about cloning humans?

C: Research Activities

Look at the chart and answer the questions on the next page.

PET OWNERSHIP INTERNATIONALLY   GfK

Percentage of people living with different pets in 22 countries

50% 39% 11% 6% USA   Argentina 66% 32% 8% 7%

27% 27% 9% 4% UK   Australia 39% 29% 13% 10%

12% 15% 16% 20% Turkey   Belgium 29% 33% 15% 8%

22% 28% 6% 3% Sweden   Average   Brazil 58% 28% 7% 11%
                        across all countries
37% 23% 9% 11% Spain   Canada 33% 35% 9% 4%

20% 6% 7% 1% South Korea   **33% 23% 12% 6%**   China 25% 10% 17% 5%

29% 57% 11% 9% Russia   Czech Republic 38% 26% 14% 8%

45% 32% 12% 7% Poland   France 29% 41% 12% 5%

25% 26% 11% 7% Netherlands   Germany 21% 29% 9% 6%

64% 24% 10% 10% Mexico   Hong Kong 14% 10% 14% 3%

17% 14% 9% 2% Japan   Italy 39% 34% 11% 8%

Source: GfK survey among 27,000+ Internet users (ages 15+) in 22 countries – multiple answers possible – rounded

1. Which country has the highest percentage of dog ownership in the world?
2. Which country has the highest percentage of cat ownership in the world?
3. In which countries is cat ownership greater than dog ownership?
4. In which country are birds the most common pet?
5. Which country has the highest percentage of fish ownership in the world?
6. Are any of the results surprising?

B EIJING — Garlic was dead, and there was nothing Huang Yu could do. So on a cold winter day, he buried his cat's body in a park close to his home.

Hours later, still heartbroken, the 22-year-old businessman recalled an article he had read on dog cloning in China. What if someday he could bring Garlic back to life? "In my heart, Garlic is irreplaceable," said Mr. Huang, who dug up his British shorthair, wrapped it carefully and placed it in his refrigerator in preparation for cloning him. "Garlic didn't leave anything for future generations, so I could only choose to clone."

That thought led him to Sinogene, a commercial pet-cloning company in Beijing. Roughly $35,000 and seven months later, Sinogene produced what China's official news media declared to be the country's first cloned cat — and another sign of the country's emergence as a power in cloning and genetics.

It also suggests that China could turn pet cloning into a viable business. The size of China's domestic pet market is expected to reach $28.2 billion this year, up nearly one-fifth from 2018, according to Gouminwang, a pet consultancy in Beijing. The country already has 55 million pet dogs and 44 million pet cats, and demand for cats is accelerating.

Pet cloning is not confined to China — Barbra Streisand famously declared last year that two of her dogs are clones — and people have been cloning cats for years. But Garlic is the first cat cloned by China, solidifying its position among major cloning nations, which include the United States, Britain and South Korea.

Mi Jidong, Sinogene's chief executive, said the company decided to start cloning pets in 2015 after conducting a survey of roughly 1,000 people that showed there was demand. The company has cloned more than 40 dogs, including schnauzers, Pomeranians and Malteses, at a cost of about $53,000 each, some as pets and others for medical research.

7　**British shorthair** 猫の品種名.

11　**commercial**　「営利目的の」

15　**power**　「大国」

22　**Barbra Streisand** 「バーブラ・ストライサンド」アメリカの歌手・女優.

5

10

15

20

25

30

It charges more for dogs than cats because the window for harvesting a dog's eggs is very small, according to Mr. Mi. He said more than 100 people had stored the DNA samples of their pets in anticipation of creating clones.

Sinogene's yearlong effort to clone a cat was motivated by market research that showed that cats are becoming increasingly popular in China, said Mr. Mi.

China's genetics know-how is growing rapidly. Ever since Chinese scientists cloned a female goat in 2000, they have succeeded in producing the world's first primate clones, monkeys, and creating superstrong dogs by tinkering with their genes. Last year, the country stunned the world after a Chinese scientist announced that he had created the world's first genetically edited babies.

Pet cloning is largely unregulated and controversial, but in China the barriers are especially low. Many Chinese people do not think that using animals for medical research or cosmetics testing is cruel, or that pet cloning is potentially problematic. There are also no laws against animal cruelty.

"It satisfies the owner's spiritual needs and increases happiness," said Wang Chuduan, a professor at China Agricultural University in Beijing. "There is a market demand. So what's the problem?"

Sinogene has bigger ambitions than cats and dogs. It is cloning a horse, and Mr. Mi said his next big goal was to clone endangered animals, including pandas and the South China tiger.

Critics contend that pet cloning is inhumane. It is not clear what will happen to the resulting animals, or the impact when they mix

Garlic's clone, Garlic.   Yan Cong for The New York Times
写真：The New York Times/Redux/ アフロ

1　gene pool　「遺伝子プール」遺伝子の供給源.

3　bioethicist　「生命倫理学者」

with the broader gene pool. The money could be better spent on caring for existing animals, the critics say.

Jessica Pierce, a bioethicist at the University of Colorado Denver, cites the use of cats as surrogate mothers to produce clones, which she said was "similar to the harm that you would impose on a woman whose only purpose in life is to be a breeding machine for man."

"The cat has no intrinsic value," Dr. Pierce said. "It's used as an object, as a means to somebody's end."

To clone Garlic, scientists implanted skin cells from Mr. Huang's original cat into eggs harvested from other cats. Forty cloned embryos were implanted into four surrogate mother cats. That produced three pregnancies, two of which were miscarriages, said Chen Benchi, head of Sinogene's medical experiments team.

Scientists outside China have not yet inspected Garlic, who was born on July 21. But the company's chief scientist, Lai Liangxue, has had his cloning research published in the respected journals Nature and Science.

18　Nature　イギリスの学術雑誌.
Science　アメリカの学術雑誌.

20　The Handmaid's Tale → Note 2

A visit to Sinogene's laboratory on the outskirts of Beijing offered scenes out of something like a feline version of "The Handmaid's Tale." Garlic's clone, a gray-and-white kitten, snoozed with his surrogate mother, a different breed from Garlic. He later played with a fur ball while three pregnant surrogate cats watched from cages. The new Garlic is scheduled to stay at Sinogene's laboratory for another month for observation before he is sent to Mr. Huang.

In his first meeting with the new Garlic in August, Mr. Huang found that cloning had not produced an exact copy of his former pet. The clone is missing a patch of black fur that graced Garlic's chin. Sinogene said that clones might show slight differences in fur or eye color and that an outside firm had proved the DNA matched.

31　outside firm　「社外企業」

"If I tell you I wasn't disappointed, then I would be lying to you," Mr. Huang said. "But I'm also willing to accept that there are certain situations in which there are limitations to the technology."

35　artificial intelligence　「人工知能」

Mr. Mi said that it may be possible to use artificial intelligence to transplant the memories of the original pet to the cloned one, but it was not something his company would try to do yet.

"It's a way to imagine the future," he said.

Notes

1 the impact when ... the broader gene pool の部分は，クローンを作り出す過程で元の猫とは違う品種の猫を利用する可能性があることから，異種同志の遺伝子が自然発生的にではなく，人間の意図によって混じり合う懸念をさしていると思われる．

2 The Handmaid's Tale（侍女の物語）は近未来を舞台のSFディストピア小説で映画化もされた．生殖能力のある女性の数が少なくなり，彼女たちが「侍女」という役割を与えられ子供を産む道具として支配者に仕え，常に監視された生活を強いられるというストーリー．

Post-reading

A: Word Match

Match the compounds to their description

1. Future generations		a. The head director of a company.
2. Domestic pet market		b. The use of animals to study the skin and health reactions to makeup products.
3. Chief executive		c. Relating to the wants and necessities of the human mind, aspirations and beliefs.
4. Genetically edited babies		d. The next and distant descendants in the line of ancestry.
5. Primate clones		e. Mammals threatened with extinction.
6. Cosmetic testing		f. A female whose sole purpose is the endless production of babies.
7. Potentially problematic		g. Genetic copies of mammals most closely related to humans, such as monkeys and apes.
8. Animal cruelty		h. Of worth in and of itself, not for another reason.
9. Spiritual needs		i. Infants whose DNA has been selected, deleted or added to, usually to remove hereditary defects.
10. Endangered animals		j. Microscopic masses of protoplasm involved in the production of flesh.
11. Surrogate mothers		k. Possibility of causing trouble.
12. Breeding machine		l. Causing physical and psychological harm to and torture of mammals.
13. Intrinsic value		m. Females who carry and give birth to another female's inseminated eggs.
14. Skin cells		n. The selling and buying of animals for private homes within a country.

B: Comprehension Questions

1. What did Huang Yu do when his irreplaceable cat, Garlic, died?
2. What is the size of the domestic pet market in China?
3. What are the 4 major cloning nations in the world?
4. How many dogs has the cloning company Sinogene cloned?
5. What other mammals have Chinese scientists cloned or genetically edited?

6. Why is it easy for Chinese scientists to do cloning in China?
7. What are Sinogene's bigger ambitions?
8. What do critics say about pet cloning?
9. To clone Garlic many cats were used. What do the numbers forty, four, three, two and one refer to?
10. What may be possible in the future using artificial intelligence?

C: Discussion Questions

1. After reading the article, what do you think of cloning pets?
2. Would you like to clone your own pet when it dies?
3. Do animals have rights like humans?
4. Is owning pets inherently wrong or is it a good thing?
5. Are there laws against animal cruelty in Japan?
6. What do you think of animal activists who, for example, free disease-free pigs from their pens, or block whaling ships from hunting whales?
7. What do you think of animal testing for medicine, or for cosmetics?

D: Research Questions

1. What was the first cloned animal in the world and where was it cloned?
2. Name all 10 kinds of animals that have been cloned in the world.
3. What country in the world has banned the commercial buying and selling of pets in pet shops?
4. Where do the people from this country get their pets?
5. Name 5 animal rights organizations in the world.
6. What organization from what country has repeatedly tried to block Japanese whaling?
7. Which cosmetic company(ies) refuse to make products that involve animal testing?
8. Look at the chart on the next page. Research online to fill in the grey blanks on the chart.

THE CLONING PROCESS

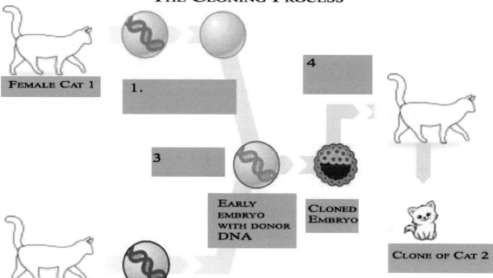

FEMALE CAT 1

1.

4

3

EARLY EMBRYO WITH DONOR DNA

CLONED EMBRYO

CLONE OF CAT 2

FEMALE CAT 2

2

VI

The Future Horizons of Foods

Unit 11

The World Wastes Tons of Food. A Grocery 'Happy Hour' Is One Answer

By David Segal   Sept. 8, 2019

A: Crossword

Match the words in the Word Bank to their descriptions to fill in the crossword.

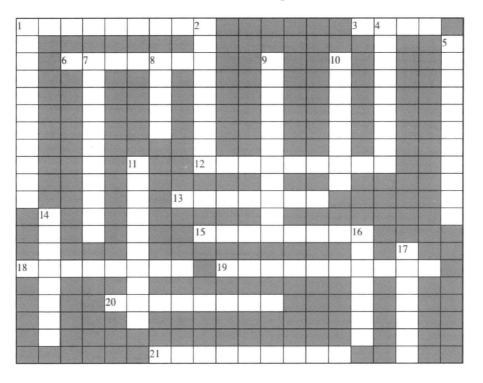

Word Bank

Acres	Advertising	Bargain	Charity	Consumption	Convivial
Director	Donated	Eliminated	Emit	Expiration	Ingredients
Landfills	Marketing	Merchants	Methane	Momentum	Past-due*
Regulars	Standardize	Start-ups*	Ventures		

*Include hyphen when filling in crossword.

Across

1. (adj.) Fond of feasting drinking and good company.
3. (v.) Let out. expel.
6. (n.) An advantageous purchase. Cheap deal.
12. (n.) A new company, usually in the tech industry.
13. (n.) Generosity and helpfulness towards the needy, poor, and suffering.
15. (n.) Strength or forced gained by motion or by a series of events.
18. (n.) Customers who frequent a shop or place everyday, or very often.
19. (n.) End of something. Finish. Release breath. Die.
20. (n.) Business enterprises involving chance, risk or danger.
21. (n.) The technique and process of promoting, selling and distributing a product or service.

Down

1. (n.) The act of using, eating up, drinking up goods and foods.
2. (n.) Places where garbage is dumped and covered with soil.
4. (n.) Buyers and sellers of goods for profit. Retail Storekeepers.
5. (n.) Something part of any mixture. E.G. Food for a recipe.
7. (n.) The action, usually in business, of calling public attention to your event, product or service.
8. (n.) A unit of area used in U.S and England equal to 4047 square meters.
9. (v.) To establish regularity, consistency.
10. (idiom) Food that is no longer edible or safe to eat.
11. (v.) Simple past. Got rid of. Stopped. Put an end to. Removed.
14. (n.) Head of a group or company.
16. (n.) A colorless, flammable gas made from decomposing organic matter.
17. (v) Simple Past. Given.

B: Discussion Questions

1. Have you worked in a restaurant, convenience store or supermarket?
2. Did you notice any food being wasted? Was it a lot?
3. What do you think could be done about it to reduce waste?
4. How about at home? Do you throw out much food at home?
5. What can we do to reduce waste at home?
6. Do you read expiration dates on packaging when you buy food?

C: Research Activities

1. Look at the pie chart. Which is the largest category of waste in the world?

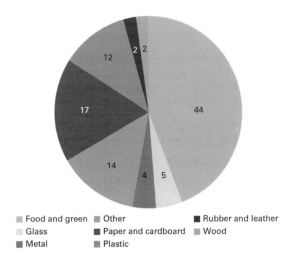

2. Look at the chart below. Which country is the largest waster of food?
3. How does Japan rank in terms of food waste?

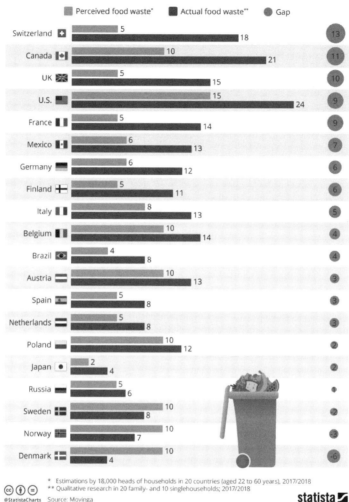

Households Waste More Food Than Estimated
Perceived and actual food waste in households per country (in %)

■ Perceived food waste*　■ Actual food waste**　● Gap

Country	Perceived	Actual	Gap
Switzerland	5	18	13
Canada	10	21	11
UK	5	15	10
U.S.	15	24	9
France	5	14	9
Mexico	6	13	7
Germany	6	12	6
Finland	5	11	6
Italy	8	13	5
Belgium	10	14	4
Brazil	4	8	4
Austria	10	13	3
Spain	5	8	3
Netherlands	5	8	3
Poland	10	12	2
Japan	2	4	2
Russia	5	6	1
Sweden	10	8	-2
Norway	10	7	-3
Denmark	10	4	-6

* Estimations by 18,000 heads of households in 20 countries (aged 22 to 60 years), 2017/2018
** Qualitative research in 20 family- and 10 singlehouseholds; 2017/2018
@StatistaCharts　Source: Movinga

statista

1　**happy hour**
「ハッピーアワー」
→ Note 1
1　**S-market**　フィンラ
ンドのスーパーマー
ケットチェーン.
3　**liquor aisle**　「酒
売り場」

10　**slashed**　「大幅に
値下げされた」

HELSINKI, Finland — "Happy hour" at the S-market store in the working-class neighborhood of Vallila happens far from the liquor aisles and isn't exactly convivial. Nobody is here for drinks or a good time. They're looking for a steep discount on a slab of pork.

Or a chicken, or a salmon fillet, or any of a few hundred items that are hours from their midnight expiration date. Food that is nearly unsellable goes on sale at every one of S-market's 900 stores in Finland, with prices that are already reduced by 30 percent slashed to 60 percent off at exactly 9 p.m. It's part of a two-year campaign to reduce food waste that company executives in this famously bibulous country decided to call "happy hour" in the hopes of drawing in regulars, like any decent bar.

"I've gotten quite hooked on this," said Kasimir Karkkainen, 27, as he browsed the meat section in the Vallila S-market. It was 9:15 and he had grabbed a container of pork mini-ribs and two pounds of shrink-wrapped pork tenderloin. Total cost after the price drop: the equivalent of $4.63.

About one-third of the food produced and packaged for human consumption is lost or wasted, according to the Food and Agriculture Organization of the United Nations. That equals 1.3 billion tons a year, worth nearly $680 billion. The figures represent more than just a disastrous misallocation of need and want, given that 10 percent of people in the world are chronically undernourished. All that excess food, scientists say, contributes to climate change.

From 8 to 10 percent of greenhouse gas emissions are related to food lost during harvest and production or wasted by consumers, a recent report by the Intergovernmental Panel on Climate Change found. Landfills of rotting food emit methane, a gas that is roughly 25 times more harmful than carbon dioxide. And to harvest and transport all that wasted food requires billions of acres of arable land, trillions of gallons of water and vast amounts of fossil fuels.

For consumers, cutting back on food waste is one of the few personal habits that can help the planet. But a lot of people who fret about their carbon footprint aren't sweating the vegetables and rump steak they toss into the garbage.

"There's been a lot of focus on energy," said Paul Behrens, a professor in energy and environmental change at the University of Leiden in the Netherlands. "But climate change is as much a land issue and a food issue as anything else."

Reducing waste is a challenge because selling as much food as possible is an ingrained part of all-you-can-eat cultures. Persuading merchants to promote and profit from "food rescue" is not so obvious.

"Consumers are paying for the food, and who wants to reduce that?" said Toine Timmermans, director of the United Against Food Waste Foundation, a nonprofit in the Netherlands. "Who profits from reducing food waste?"

A growing number of supermarkets, restaurants and start-ups — many based in Europe — are trying to answer that question. The

---

Glossary (margin notes):

2 **regular** 「常連客」
3 **get hooked on ~** 「~に夢中になる，ハマる」
6 **shrink-wrapped** 「収縮包装の」
9 **the Food and Agriculture Organization of the United Nations** 「国際連合食料農業機関」
12 **misallocation** 「配分の間違い」
13 **given that ~** 「~を考慮すると」
18 **the Inter-governmental Panel on Climate Change** 「気候変動に関する政府間パネル」
25 **carbon footprint** 「CO$_2$排出量」
    sweat 「気にする」
32 **all-you-can-eat culture** 「食べ放題の文化」
34 **obvious** 「(聞いて) すぐわかる，容易に理解できる」
39 **start-up** 「新興企業」

United States is another matter.

"Food waste might be a uniquely American challenge because many people in this country equate quantity with a bargain," said Meredith Niles an assistant professor in food systems at the University of Vermont. "Look at the number of restaurants that advertise their supersized portions."

Nine of the 10 United States supermarket chains that were assessed by the nonprofit Center for Biological Diversity last year were given a C grade or lower on food-waste issues. Only Walmart did better, largely for its efforts to standardize date labels and to educate staffers and customers.

Some of the most promising food waste efforts are apps that connect food sellers to food buyers. Among the most popular is Too Good to Go, a company based in Copenhagen, with 13 million users and contracts with 25,000 restaurants and bakeries in 11 countries. Consumers pay about one-third of the sticker price for items, most of which goes to the retailer, with a small percentage paid to the app.

In Denmark, food rescue has attained the scale and momentum of a cultural movement, one with its own intellectual godmother: Selina Juul, a graphic designer who immigrated from Russia at the age of 13.

"I came from a country where there was a fear that we wouldn't have food on the table tomorrow," she said. "When we emigrated, I had never seen so much food. I was shocked. Then I was shocked again when I saw how much food people wasted."

In 2008, at the age of 28, she started a Facebook group called Stop Wasting Food. Within weeks, she was being interviewed on the radio. Soon after that, she came to the attention of Anders Jensen, the buying director at REMA 1000, the largest supermarket chain in Denmark.

"I was on a business trip to Scotland and I read about Selina in a newspaper," Mr. Jensen recalls. "Around that time, we learned that every Dane was throwing out 63 kilos of food per year and I was sitting in this airport thinking, she's right."

After the two met in a Copenhagen cafe, REMA 1000 eliminated in-store bulk discounts. As of 2008, there would be no more three hams for the price of two, or any variations on that theme. "It exploded in the media because it was the first time a retailer said, 'It's O.K. if we sell less,'" Mr. Jensen said.

REMA 1000 and Ms. Juul recognize that there is a limit to how much one company can do to reduce waste. Consciousness raising was necessary. So Ms. Juul has enlisted famous Danes to join her cause.

She's co-writing a book on cooking with leftovers with Princess Marie, who worked in advertising and marketing before marrying into the Danish royal family. Celebrity chefs, like Rene Redzepi, have spread the word. Mette Frederiksen, the current prime minister, even made it a campaign issue this year.

In Finland, reducing food waste has yet to become a political issue, but it is a selling point for at least one restaurant. Every dish on the menu of Loop is made from past-due ingredients donated by grocery stores and bakeries. Donations vary, so Loop's chefs have no idea what they'll be making until they walk into the restaurant's kitchen.

"It's like an episode of 'Master Chef' every day," said Johanna Kohvakka, founder of the nonprofit From Waste to Taste, which operates Loop. "But we try to make every dish look great."

Ms. Kohvakka says Loop turns a profit and could serve as a model for similar ventures. Executives at S-market in Finland make no such claims about their happy hour. Mika Lyytikainen, an S-market vice president, explained that the program simply reduces its losses.

"When we sell at 60 percent off, we don't earn any money, but we earn more than if the food was given to charity," he said. "On the other hand, it's now possible for every Finn to buy very cheap food in our stores."

It's not unusual to find groups of S-market shoppers milling around with soon-to-be-discounted items from the shelves and waiting for the clock to strike at 9. "I've done that," Mr. Karkkainen said, as he headed for the exits with his pork mini ribs.

Some Finns, it seems, haven't fully embraced S-market's anti-waste ethos. Harri Hartikainen, 71, was shopping one evening in Vallila and considered a 60 percent off box of Kansas City-style grilled chicken wings. "I've never tried these before," he said, dropping them into his shopping basket. "But it's so cheap, if I don't like it, I can just throw it out."

---

4 **cause** 「(社会運動などの) 主義主張, 理想」
5 **Princess Marie** 「メアリー皇太子妃」
7 **Mette Frederiksen** 「メッテ・フレデリクセン」 → Note 2
9 **campaign issue** 「選挙運動の争点」
10 **have yet to ~** 「まだ～していない」
12 **past-due** 「期限を過ぎた」
16 **Master Chef** 「マスターシェフ」 → Note 3
19 **turn a profit** 「利益を出す」
21 **such claims** 「これこれの損害が出たとの支払い請求」
29 **soon-to-be-discounted** 「まもなく安くなる」

Notes

1 本来ハッピーアワーというのは，レストランやバーなどの飲食店でビールやワインなどの酒類がお得な値段で飲める時間帯のことをいう．飲食には少し早い夕方の時間帯に人を呼び込むためのサー

ビスとして行う店が多い.

2　メッテ・フレデリクセンは社会民主党の代表で 2019 年の総選挙で首相に就任した. デンマークでは 2 人目の女性首相で, なおかつ 41 歳という最年少で就任した首相でもある.

3　マスターシェフは料理の腕前を競うリアリティ番組で 1990 年にイギリスで放映が始まった. 素人料理人がその場で与えられたテーマと時間制限の中, マスターシェフの称号を目指して競うもので, ミシュランの星を持つシェフなどがジャッジを務める. その後アメリカを初め世界各国で同じような番組が作られ, プロの料理人たちが参加するものや子供たちの大会, 有名人たちのバトルなどのバリエーションが現れた.

Post-reading

A: Word Match

Match the compounds to their description

1. Happy hour		a. A distribution of goods or skills that results in a terrible situation.
2. Expiration date		b. The amount of CO_2 a person or species leaves in the environment.
3. Food waste		c. CO_2 and methane that are expelled into the atmosphere.
4. Disastrous misallocation		d. Coal, oil or natural gas formed in the ground from plant and animal remains and used to propel cars.
5. Chronically undernourished		e. The saving/use of edibles from the garbage.
6. Greenhouse gas emissions		f. A sales promotion event usually at a bar.
7. Carbon dioxide		g. Hanging about. Loitering.
8. Fossil fuels		h. An endless or ever repeating period of famine or severe lack of food.
9. Carbon footprint		i. Extra large serving of food.
10. Supersized portions		j. The day after which a product is no longer safe to eat or use.
11. Food rescue		k. A colorless gas formed by animal respiration, or decomposition of plants and is absorbed by living plants. It is responsible for much of the greenhouse effect.
12. Sticker price		l. The letting out of flammable, odorless, colorless gas, usually through decomposition.
13. Milling around		m. Edible products thrown in the garbage.
14. Emit methane		n. The cost marked on a product in a store.

B: Comprehension Questions

1. What is the S-market in Helsinki Finland selling at its happy hour?
2. At what time and by how much cheaper do nearly unsellable items go for?
3. How much of the food produced and packaged for human consumption is lost or

wasted and at what cost according to the Food and Agriculture Organization?

4. What percentage of greenhouse gas emissions are caused by food lost during harvest and production, and food wasted by consumers?
5. What is emitted by food left rotting in landfills?
6. What is one of the few personal habits that consumers can change to reduce their carbon footprint?
7. Why are Americans especially challenged in reducing food waste according to Meredith Niles, assistant professor in food systems at the University of Vermont?
8. Why was Walmart the only one of ten supermarket chains that were positively assessed by the Center for Biological Diversity?
9. How many people use the Too Good to Go food app that connects food sellers and buyers?
10. Who is the godmother of the food rescue movement in Denmark?
11. What inspired her to start her Facebook group Stop Wasting Food?
12. What is special about the dishes at Loop restaurant?

C: Discussion Questions

1. Do you eat leftovers at your house or throw them away?
2. Would you eat at a restaurant like Loop that uses only leftovers?
3. Do you care about expiration dates on food?
4. Have you ever eaten food that is past its due-date?
5. When there are so many people starving in the world, why do you think there is so much wasted food?
6. What can we do as individuals to stop waste?
7. What should stores and each country do to limit waste?

D: Research Questions

1. How many tons of food are wasted every year?
2. How many people are malnourished in the world?
3. List ways in which we may stop waste at home.
4. List ways in which stores and companies may reduce waste.
5. List things the government should do.

Unit 12

Fake Meat vs. Real Meat

By Anahad O'Connor   Dec. 3, 2019

Pre-reading

A: Crossword

Match the words in the Word Bank to their descriptions to fill in the crossword.

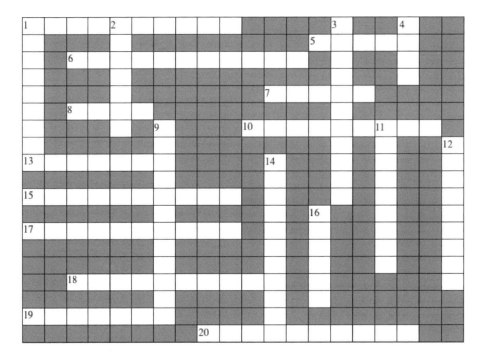

Word Bank

Alternatives	Appear	Beet	Cholesterol	Derivative	Disrupt	Financial
Heme	Imitation	Labeled	Legumes	Millennials	Misleading	Niche
Op-ed*	Popularity	Processed	Replicated	Sacrifice	Substitutes	Vegetarian

*Include hyphen when filling in crossword.

Across

1. (n.) The quality of being liked by many people.
5. (n.) A specialized market.
6. (n.) People or things that take the place or function of others.
7. (n.) Short for opposite editorial, referring to the page opposite the editorial of a newspaper.
8. (n.) A root vegetable that is used for food, a source of sugar and a dye due to its red color.
10. (adj.) Relating to the system of money, credit, investments and banking.
13. (v.) Throw into disorder. Break apart.
15. (n.) A person who does not eat meat.
17. (v.) Past Participle. Duplicated. Copied.
18. (n.) Something that comes from another substance.
19. (n.) Fruits or seeds of the peas and bean family. Any vegetable used for food.
20. (v.) Present participle. Giving a false impression.

Down

1. (adj.) Something that has undergone treatment, often referring to prepared foods that include many additives.
2. (v.) Simple Past. To identify a person by a characteristic or type. Described.
3. (n.) Generation Y. People born between 1981 and 1996.
4. (n.) An iron containing compound made from soy with a red pigment.
9. (n.) Propositions, situations or things that offer choices beyond what is presently accepted.
11. (n.) A counterfeit, a fake copy.
12. (v.) To give up something in order to obtain something else.
14. (n.) An animal steroid that controls membrane fluidity.
16. (v.) Look like, seem like.

B: Discussion Questions

1. Do you like meat?
2. How often do you eat meat each week/day?
3. What do you eat most? Beef, chicken, fish, or pork?
4. Could you give up eating meat for health or environmental reasons?
5. If you had to give up meat, what would you replace it with?
6. Have you ever eaten fake meat, like a tofu hotdog, or veggie burger?
7. Did you like it? Or would you like to try some?

C: Research Activities

Look at the map below and answer questions 1-3 on the next page.

Where Meat Consumption Is Highest & Lowest

Total per capita meat consumption worldwide in 2014 (in kg)*

0–10
10–20
20–40
40–60
60–80
80–100
100–120
No data

* 2014 is the latest year data is available. Excludes seafood.
@StatistaCharts Source: UN Food and Agriculture Organization via Our World in Data

statista

1. Which 3 countries are the biggest meat eaters?
2. Name 3 of the smallest meat eating countries.
3. How many kilos of meat do people in Japan eat each year?
4. Look at the chart below. What are the top 3 alternative meat eating countries?

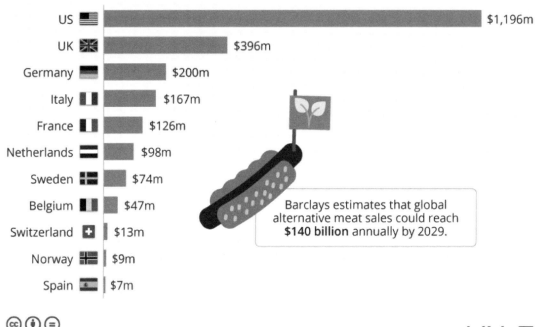

Alternative Meat Market Poised for Growth
Estimated meat substitute sales in selected countries in 2018

US — $1,196m
UK — $396m
Germany — $200m
Italy — $167m
France — $126m
Netherlands — $98m
Sweden — $74m
Belgium — $47m
Switzerland — $13m
Norway — $9m
Spain — $7m

Barclays estimates that global alternative meat sales could reach **$140 billion** annually by 2029.

@StatistaCharts   Sources: Barclays, Euromonitor

statista

The meat industry has a warning for consumers: Beware of plant-based meat.

That is the message behind a marketing campaign by the Center for Consumer Freedom, a public relations firm whose financial supporters have included meat producers and others in the food industry. In recent weeks the group has placed full-page ads in The New York Times and other newspapers raising health concerns about plant-based meat substitutes like the Impossible Burger and the Beyond Burger, which are designed to look, taste and even appear to bleed like real meat.

The ads call them "ultra-processed imitations" with numerous ingredients. "What's hiding in your plant-based meat?" asks one ad featuring a sad face made of two patties and sausage. Another directs readers to a site that compares plant-based burgers to dog food. In November, the group's managing director, Will Coggin, wrote an opinion piece in USA Today that labeled fake meats as ultra-processed foods that can spur weight gain. A few days later, the center's executive director, Rick Berman, wrote an op-ed in The Wall Street Journal criticizing plant-based meats as highly processed and no healthier than meat. Its headline: "'Plant-Based Meat' Is All Hat and No Cattle."

Impossible Foods, which makes a popular plant-based burger, said the campaign was misleading and fear-mongering. The company says plant-based meat alternatives are better for consumers and better for the planet, requiring less land and water and producing fewer greenhouse gas emissions than meat from cattle. The new "disinformation" campaign, they say, is a sign that Impossible Foods' mission — to disrupt the meat industry and replace animals in the food system — is working.

Unlike other vegetarian meat substitutes, the new plant-based burgers are winning over meat lovers. The market research firm NPD Group says that 90 percent of the customers purchasing them are meat-eaters who believe the products are more healthful and better for the environment, said Darren Seifer, an analyst at NPD, which recently predicted that plant-based meats will have staying power because of their popularity with millennials.

"The two big brands, Beyond and Impossible, have replicated the burger experience without having to sacrifice the taste of the burger," he said. "So now a lot of consumers feel like they have a healthier option, they are reducing the amount of meat they consume, and they just feel better about that."

But are plant-based meats really better for you than meat? It depends on how you eat them, said Dr. Frank Hu, chairman of the nutrition department at the Harvard T.H. Chan School of Public Health. Replacing a hamburger with a plant burger is not an improvement in diet quality if you chase it with French fries and a sugar-laden soda, Dr. Hu said.

In August, Dr. Hu, along with a group of health and climate experts, published a report in JAMA that explored whether plant-based meats can be part of a "healthy low-carbon diet." Studies show that replacing red meat with nuts, legumes and other plant foods can lower mortality and chronic disease risk, but it's not possible to extrapolate that processed burgers made with purified soy or pea protein will have the same health benefits, said Dr. Hu.

2　**opinion piece**「意見記事」

4　**op-ed**「特集記事」

7　**all hat and no cattle**「格好だけで中身がない」→ Note 2

10　**meat alternative**「代用肉」

17　**win over**「味方に引き入れる」

21　**staying power**「持久力」

22　**millennials**「ミレニアル世代」主に 1981～1996 年生まれの人をさす.

30　**Harvard T. H. Chan School of Public Health**「ハーバード公衆衛生大学院」

32　**chase ~ with ...**「… で~の口直しをする」

33　**sugar-laden**「砂糖たっぷりの」

35　**JAMA**　医学雑誌

36　**low-carbon**「CO_2 排出量の少ない」

37　**red meat**「赤身の肉」牛肉や羊肉など生の状態で赤い肉.

39　**purified**「精製した」

—105—

Impossible Foods and Beyond Meat say the building blocks of their burgers are plants. The Beyond Burger has about 18 ingredients, including purified pea protein, coconut and canola oils, rice protein, potato starch and beet juice extract for coloring. Beyond Meat says it uses no genetically modified or artificially produced ingredients.

The Impossible Burger is made with similar basic ingredients but it gets its protein largely from soy and potato, and it uses an iron-containing compound from soy called heme to enhance the burger's meaty flavor. Both products use methylcellulose, a plant derivative commonly used in sauces and ice cream, as a binder.

Compared to a beef patty, the Impossible and Beyond burgers have similar amounts of protein and calories, with less saturated fat and no cholesterol. They also contain fiber; real meat does not. But compared to real beef, the two plant-based burgers are considerably higher in sodium, containing about 16 percent of the recommended daily value. An uncooked four-ounce beef patty has about 75 milligrams of sodium, compared to 370 milligrams of sodium in the Impossible Burger and 390 milligrams in the Beyond Burger.

This fall, Burger King said it had its most successful quarter in four years, driven by sales of its plant-based Impossible Whopper. Dunkin' Donuts announced it was rolling out a breakfast sandwich made with Beyond Meat sausages in 9,000 of its stores. More than 50,000 grocery stores and restaurants, including fast food chains like Subway, White Castle, KFC and Carl's Jr., carry products from Beyond Meat or Impossible Foods.

Despite the popularity of plant-based burgers, beef burgers are still overwhelmingly the more popular choice at restaurants. Americans purchased 6.4 billion beef burgers at quick service restaurants during the 12 months that ended in May, compared to 228 million plant-based burgers in the same period.

While meat consumption in America is at an all-time high, many Americans have shifted from eating beef to poultry. In the past three decades, beef intake has fallen by about a third, while chicken intake has more than doubled and pork intake has remained fairly steady. Studies show that cost, convenience and health concerns are among the top reasons Americans have cut back on beef.

Meat producers are taking the fight against fake meat to lawmakers. At least 25 states have introduced bills making it illegal to use the words "beef" or "meat" on products made from plant

	ingredients or cultured meat that is grown in a lab. Missouri became the first state to pass such a law last year, which was initially proposed by the Missouri Cattlemen's Association.

ingredients or cultured meat that is grown in a lab. Missouri became the first state to pass such a law last year, which was initially proposed by the Missouri Cattlemen's Association.

In October, Representative Roger Marshall, a Republican from Kansas, introduced a federal bill that would require companies to put the word "imitation" on their plant-based meat products. The bill calls for the products to carry a statement on their packages "that clearly indicates the product is not derived from or does not contain meat."

Dr. Marshall, an obstetrician, said he introduced the bill after hearing from constituents. Patients of his told him they were confused about the health benefits of plant-based beef substitutes, and beef producers told him they were frustrated that the products are sold in grocery stores next to ground beef. "Kansas has a very large beef industry and they said, 'Why are we allowing this fake meat in the meat department?'" he said.

Mr. Brown, the chief executive of Impossible Foods, said his company's mission is not to convince consumers that the Impossible Burger is the most nutritious food they can eat. It is simply to persuade people who want a "cow burger" to eat an Impossible Burger instead.

"The niche that this fills is not the same niche that a kale salad fills," he said. "If you're hungry for a burger and you want something that's better for you and better for the planet that delivers everything you want from a burger, then this is a great product. But if you're hungry for a salad, eat a salad."

Notes

1 Impossible Burger と Beyond Burger は, それぞれアメリカの Impossible Foods 社, Beyond Meat 社が開発した人工肉を使ったバーガー.

2 all hat and no cattle とは, 直訳するならば「帽子を被っているだけで牛は扱っていない」ということ. カウボーイハットを被ってはいるものの, それは格好だけで本物のカウボーイではない, つまり「見た目を装うだけで中身は偽物だ」というような意味で使われる.

3 培養肉とは, 動物そのものの肉ではなく, 動物から採取した細胞組織を培養することによって人工的に作り出された肉のことをいう.

Post-reading

A: Word Match

Match the compounds to their description

1. Marketing campaign		a. Foods involving various treatments and countless ingredients including chemicals.
2. Financial supporters		b. Trying to benefit politically or financially from scaring people.
3. Health concerns		c. Worries about one's body.
4. Ultra-processed		d. Emitting very little CO_2
5. Opinion piece		e. Made with chemicals and additives rather than with natural ingredients.
6. Fear-mongering		f. A choice that is better for one's body.
7. Disinformation campaign		g. A series of events designed to increase sales.
8. Healthier option		h. Food with altered DNA.
9. Low-carbon		i. Laboratory, in vitro grown cellular structures made to look like animal products.
10. Chronic disease		j. Unhealthy animal and plant fats that are so full of hydrogen molecules they solidify when not heated.
11. Genetically modified		k. Companies or individuals who provide money for a project.
12. Artificially produced		l. A sickness that continues or reoccurs all your life.
13. Saturated fat		m. An article in a news paper that is not a report, but an individual view on a subject.
14. Cultured meat		n. A series of events or articles created to purposely mislead people, and promote false knowledge.

B: Comprehension Questions

1. What is the meat industry warning consumers about?
2. What is wrong with plant-based meats according to the Center for Consumer Freedom?
3. What did Impossible Foods reply to the Center for Consumer Freedom's campaign?
4. Why are plant-based meats better for the planet?
5. Which groups of people are plant-based meats winning over and staying popular with?
6. What do consumers of Beyond and Impossible feel better about?
7. When is eating plant-based meats not healthier for you according to T.H Chan?
8. What ingredients do these plant-based burgers include?
9. What ingredients do they not include?
10. In terms of amounts of proteins and minerals etc., how are these burgers similar and how different to a real beef patty?
11. How many sales of beef burgers were there compared to plant-based burgers?

12. What kinds of meat are Americans eating more of and which less of?

C: Discussion Questions

1. After reading this article would you consider trying some plant-based meats?
2. Would you consider switching your diet to eating less meat?
3. Were you surprised that big fast food chain stores like Burger King, Dunkin' Donuts and KFC are buying these fake meat products?
4. Do you think eating less meat is better for the environment? Why/Why not?
5. What other foods might we give up for the environment?

D: Research Questions

1. What religion first developed fake meats to please visitors?
2. What did they make the fake meats out of?
3. When did they first develop these fake meats?
4. Make a list of ingredients needed to make fake burgers at home (E.G.tofu/lentil burger)
5. Make a list of ingredients in a store bought plant-based burger.
6. What is the water footprint of beef compared to that of soy beans?
7. How many acres of land are needed for 1 cow to get the same food value from 1 acre of corn?

テキストの音声は、弊社 HP
http://www.eihosha.co.jp/
の「テキスト音声ダウンロード」の
バナーからダウンロードできます。

表紙デザイン：山本　彩

Beyond Borders
ニューヨークタイムズ世界見聞

2021 年 1 月 15 日　初　版
2023 年 2 月 28 日　2　刷

編 注 者　　喜 多　　留 女
　　　　　　K. W. Adams

発 行 者　　佐 々 木　　元

発 行 所　　株式会社　英　宝　社
〒101-0032 東京都千代田区岩本町 2-7-7
TEL 03 (5833) 5870-1 FAX 03 (5833) 5872

ISBN 978-4-269-19035-1 C1082
［製版：伊谷企画／印刷・製本：モリモト印刷株式会社］

［CD 完備（ダウンロード可）］